Project Portfolio Management
Tools and Techniques

Parviz F. Rad

Ph.D., P.E., C.C.E., PMP
Principal, Project Management Excellence
Berkeley Heights, New Jersey

Ginger Levin

D.P.A., PMP
Senior Project Management Consultant
Lecturer in Project Management, University of Wisconsin-Platteville
Lighthouse Point, Florida

IIL PUBLISHING, NEW YORK

IIL Publishing, New York titles may be purchased in bulk at a discount for educational, business, fund-raising, or sales promotional use. For information, please e-mail michelle. blackley@iil.com or call 212-515-5144.

Published by IIL Publishing, New York a division of International Institute for Learn-ing, Inc., 110 East 59th Street, 31st Floor, New York, NY 10022
www.iil.com

Publisher: Judith W. Umlas
Design: Tony Meisel

Library of Congress Cataloging-in-Publication Data available.

Rad, Parviz F.; Levin, Ginger

ISBN 0-9708276-8-7

Printed in the United States of America

I Dedicate This Book
To My Brother Fereydoon
For his lifelong support, insightful mentoring, and unparalleled wisdom
PFR

To My Husband Morris
For his continuing support and love
GL

Contents

Preface

Increasingly, projects are recognized as major components of almost every organization's work. Managing organizations by projects is no longer the exception, but rather, is the norm. Many organizations view successful projects as a competitive advantage and establish full-scale portfolio management systems to assist in ensuring project success. With an increased recognition of the project management profession, the focus of organizational attention is no longer on only one or two large, complex projects. Instead, the organizational attention is focused on the management of the collective set of all projects.

A large number of project professionals are needed for the execution of an ambitious number of projects. Further, in most organizations, there are more potential projects to pursue than there are available resources with which to pursue those projects. Thus, a formal project portfolio management (PPM) process becomes an operational necessity. It is essential that a formal PPM system be established to assist the organization in pursuing the most important projects based on an established set of criteria. Such a process is not a one-time exercise, but rather, is a dynamic process that is carefully maintained and regularly reviewed with an organizational commitment. The objective of a well-constructed PPM system is to ensure that with limited resources and available time, the organization selects the projects that facilitate its success. A prioritized list of projects can ensure that organizational objectives and portfolio priorities are in concert.

Implementing a PPM process requires a dedicated commitment from upper management, because the implementation can be a major culture change. Such a methodical approach will require an organization that is friendly toward projects. To support this kind of decision making and oversight, projects and programs must follow a consistent data collection and reporting process. A centralized view of the enterprise's projects will show their interrelationships and priorities. The result is a PPM system that is fully strategic and mission-driven. Additionally, the projects in the portfolio will be managed in an informed, rather than an ad hoc, fashion. Ideally, the management of portfolios, programs, and projects should be intertwined in a formal fashion. This formalized relationship will provide the foundation for transferring data between the teams that manage projects, programs, and portfolios. There might be an overlap of personnel between these three functions, which is more to the point that each function must have its own appropriate process for logical and methodical decisions.

This book deals with the full spectrum of PPM functions, i.e., selecting projects through formalized portfolio management and facilitating the successful execution of projects through creating a formalized, project-friendly environment. Chapter 1 of this book elaborates on the importance of portfolio management by describing formalized portfolio management. Chapter 2 describes the functions of an Enterprise Project Management Office, and the facilitation that it would bring to managing a portfolio of projects. Chapter 3 deals with practices in PPM implementation and provides guidelines, instruments, and checklists for establishing a PPM system within the organization. This chapter builds upon the Project Management Institute® (PMI) 2006 *The Standard for Portfolio Management*. Chapter 4 introduces a comprehensive project portfolio model. It describes the processes and formalized analytical structures for forming portfolios, prioritizing projects of the portfolios, and managing this collection of projects. This PPM model advocates a distinction between the metrics that describe the project deliverable, the metrics that describe the business case of the project, and the metrics that describe the financial attractiveness of the project deliverable.

Parviz F. Rad
Ginger Levin

About the Authors

Parviz F. Rad, Ph.D., P.E., C.C.E., PMP, is an independent project management consultant. He holds an MSc. from Ohio State University and a Ph.D. from Massachusetts Institute of Technology. He has over 35 years of professional experience, during which he has served in governmental, industrial, and academic capacities. He has participated in project management activities and in the development and enhancement of quantitative tools in project management in a multitude of disciplines, including software development, construction, and pharmaceutical research. He has authored or coauthored more than 60 publications in the areas of engineering and project management. Dr. Rad is a former editor of the Project Management Institute's *Project Management Journal*.

Ginger Levin, D.P.A, PMP, is a senior consultant in project management with more than 30 years of experience. She is also a lecturer for the University of Wisconsin-Platteville in its Master of Science in Project Management program and serves as the university's program specialist in project management. Dr. Levin received her doctorate in public administration and information systems technology from The George Washington University (GWU), where she received the outstanding dissertation award for her research on large organizations. She also has an M.S.A., with a concentration in information systems technology, from GWU and a B.B.A. from Wake Forest University.

Dr. Rad and Dr. Levin are also the authors of *Metrics for Project Management: Formalized Approaches* (Management Concepts), *The Advanced Project Management Office* (CRC Press), and *Achieving Project Management Success Using Virtual Teams* (J. Ross Publishing).

1. Introduction to Project Portfolio Management

Traditional project management is, by and large, a process whereby each project is approved and managed independently. In this arena, the focus is on a single project and the triple constraint—scope, time, and cost—of that project separate from other projects. Typically, the project manager is responsible for evaluating the performance of the project. At times, given the importance of the project, the project might be evaluated or reviewed at the executive level, but this review is still conducted in isolation of other projects.

By contrast, in the portfolio management environment, there is a predefined process for selecting projects and a uniform process for evaluating their success. The selection decisions, and the periodic evaluations, are made in light of the enterprise's business goals and strategies. Evaluations are conducted regularly and are based on standardized procedures. The emphasis is on ensuring that each project contributes to the overall organizational success. The project must continue to support business goals even if there are major changes in the project requirements.

Project portfolio management (PPM) is generally defined as a dynamic decision-making process, whereby a business' list of active projects is constantly updated and revised (Cooper, 2001). In this process, new projects are evaluated, selected, and prioritized; existing projects may be accelerated, killed, or deprioritized; and resources can be allocated and reallocated to the active projects. PPM can also be defined as managing a group of projects that do not share a common objective (APM, 2000). Another definition of PPM is a group of projects or programs and other work that are grouped together to facilitate effective management of that work to meet strategic business objectives (PMI, 2004). Appendix 1 includes a review of the current literature on PPM, including the highlights of the evolution history and currently accepted practices of PPM.

A full-scale PPM process goes beyond the management of multiple projects in that all of the projects in the PPM system are evaluated in concert with each other and in the light of the corporate vision and mission. Portfolio management has a broader context since it emphasizes a collective response to organizational needs during the planning and execution of these projects. Naturally, in an informed PPM environment, projects are added to the portfolio, and subtracted from it, based on their overall contributions to the corporate vision and strategic needs. Unlike traditional project management, which focused only on managing a standalone project bounded by a budget, schedule, and scope, PPM is regarded as the critical discipline for organizational success.

The overall performance of the organization is directly tied to the sophistication of the organization in managing the entire suite of projects. In turn, project management performance is partly tied to having best practices in managing projects and partly tied to strategic planning in selecting those projects.

The project life cycle generally consists of a concept phase, a planning phase, an execution phase, a monitoring and controlling phase, and a closing phase. However, the portfolio management life cycle is broader and has a different focus. It consists of identifying enterprise opportunities, selecting the projects to help fulfill these opportunities, planning and executing these projects, and continually assessing the benefits of these projects to organizational success. In many ways, project management is a subsidiary component of portfolio management as it focuses on the planning and execution of the specific selected projects of the portfolio.

The portfolio management guidelines further emphasize monitoring each project regularly to assess the project's contribution to the organization's strategic goals. This active monitoring enables corrective actions to be taken if it is noted that a project is no longer contributing to corporate needs, as originally planned. If corrective actions are insufficient in remedying the project performance problem, the project might be terminated. This decision process differs from the traditional project management approach in which, once the project is selected for execution, it does not require further examination to determine whether the project should continue to be pursued. Midstream scrutiny is essential for organizational success as it is guided by changes in overall organizational strategic direction.

Whereas immature organizations evaluate and monitor only a few projects that are considered complex or important, mature organizations evaluate all projects under way using a PPM system. Many organizations are adopting a management-by-projects approach for their work, as the benefits of formalized project management become increasingly apparent in the organization. While project management has been practiced for centuries, the recent trend is that a project management culture is permeating many organizations. The culture change is evident by the increase in membership in professional associations specializing in project management. Further, many project professionals pursue masters and doctoral level degrees in project management, and many seek professional certification in project management. More and more, project team members seek out and use sophisticated project management tools and techniques. It is anticipated that worldwide organizations will embrace, value, and utilize PPM as a major contributor to their business success.

Therefore, the goals of portfolio management include providing mechanisms and procedures that would facilitate a timely, methodical, and effective project prioritization at each of the review points and a formalized set of guidelines for managing a group of projects in a collective fashion. Portfolio management is expected to adapt, on a regular basis, to new circumstances brought on by the continual changes in organizational strategy and project attributes. PPM is a dynamic process in that all projects within the portfolio are examined, on a regular or semi-regular basis, in light of organizational missions and strategies. It is characterized by changing information, dynamic opportunities, and interdependencies among projects. Other characteristics are multiple strategic objectives, multiple business goal considerations, multiple decision makers, and multiple locations for the project team members.

In the vast majority of organizations, PPM is often nonexistent or is not effective. Only 20% of companies that are primarily engaged in research and development initiatives have a formal and consistent process of prioritizing and managing the projects in their portfolios (Cooper, 2001). The data further show that the percentage of such enlightened organizations across all industries is only around 10%.

Many organizations, especially those in a consulting or service environment, feel that such prioritization is not practicable and thus authorize all proposed projects. This is especially the case in organizations where team members, project managers, and functional managers have conflicting objectives and priorities, all of which contribute to projects over-running their cost and duration targets. Thus, if the portfolio management process is not fully in place, or is entirely nonexistent, the enterprise might be suffering significant financial losses, albeit, invisible losses. These financial losses will be incurred as a result of assigning people part time to multiple projects to give the illusion of active projects, wasted time of project managers in negotiating for more resources, and the project team spending extensive effort in dealing with the unexpected addition or subtraction of resources from outside the project. The conflicting objectives and priorities refer to the reality that a functional manager is focused on streamlined success of operational and maintenance activities, whereas a project manager is focused on success of projects, even though they both share the same resource pool.

This book deals with the full spectrum of PPM functions, i.e., selecting projects through formalized portfolio management and facilitating the successful execution of projects through creating a highly project-friendly environment.

1.1 Benefits of Project Portfolio Management

The primary benefit of a PPM system is that only the right projects will be selected and/or continued. Thus, the projects in the pipeline will be fully aligned with the strategic business goals of the enterprise. However, to some people, PPM might appear to add a level of complexity to managing projects. This notion is partially correct in that projects will no longer be conducted as isolated islands in the enterprise. In most cases, the barriers to establishing a PPM system are the magnitude of the efforts involved in changing the organizational environment and culture to support a formalized process, the possible training involved, and the initial investment necessary for the development of the required procedures and tools. On the other hand, the benefits of having a formalized and fully effective PPM system are better competitive positioning, an improvement in the effectiveness of the project teams, and a lower overall cost of projects.

A PPM system will assist the enterprise by providing the data necessary to make informed and rational decisions regarding funding of projects. To carry that one step further, if the strategic direction of the enterprise is sufficiently articulated, the portfolio management system will make those decisions on behalf of the enterprise. The PPM system will have a centralized view of all of the enterprise's projects, with the information relating to whether, and to what extent, these projects are interrelated. With this backdrop, decisions on initiating, continuing, or abandoning projects will be based on rational data and articulated logic, and not based on emotions and politics, as sometimes they can be.

PPM is a strategic and mission-driven process that is concerned with the entire enterprise as a whole. As such, the results of the PPM optimization process might not be necessarily in the best interest of a given project; rather, they are in the best interest of the enterprise. One example of such an optimization is the case where only a fraction of the required resources are assigned to a given project, with the full knowledge that reduced resources will delay the delivery of that specific project, on the premise that increasing the resource pool is not in the best interest of the enterprise, and that the resources can be used better elsewhere.

The tools and techniques that are used for this prioritization process range from the very simple to the very complex. Notwithstanding, there is a high degree of implicit judgment in many of these systems. Regardless of how successful and sophisticated the tools of PPM are, the basic output of PPM is a prioritized list of projects. This prioritization will signal that the project on top of the list is most important and should be afforded all resources that it needs.

Therefore, under this unified project management approach, all organizational projects will be related to other projects by virtue of sharing the same technical goal, by sharing the same budget pool, by sharing the same resource pool, or by contributing to the same strategic initiative. Thus, there needs to be a formalized and consistent means of collecting project information so that the data for all projects can be compared with each other and/or combined with each other.

The PPM process will probably impact the project activities by requiring that all projects and programs follow a consistent data collection and reporting methodology. Additionally, such organizationally consistent PPM procedures will provide the upper management with a detailed and informed view of all portfolios in progress. If a fully capable PPM is first implemented in one of the functional areas, then the success stories of this implementation might encourage the entire enterprise to adopt some form of a single portfolio of projects for the entire organization. A single portfolio will have the advantage of a centralized mechanism for decision making and oversight of the enterprise investments in projects.

Ideally, in a highly sophisticated organization, there will be a single portfolio that will contain all of the projects of the organization. Alternately, and depending on circumstances, there could be several portfolios of projects, where each portfolio would contain projects relating to a specific topic or to a separate functional area or business unit of the enterprise. Admittedly, having one portfolio is far more complex, and it tends to constrain the discretion that divisional vice presidents, or other people in equivalent functions, enjoy in selecting and funding projects. On the other hand, a single portfolio will elevate the project optimization from the divisional level to the enterprise level for the greater good of the entire organization.

1.2 Attributes of a Project Portfolio Management System

Ideally, the management of portfolios, programs, and projects should be intertwined in a formal fashion. Such a formalized relationship will provide the foundation for transferring data between the teams that manage projects, programs, and portfolios. Interestingly enough, there might be an overlap of personnel between these three functions, which is more to the point that each function must have its own appropriate data for logical and methodical decisions.

Usually project management activities are conducted by a project team, while the portfolio management activities are conducted by the upper management of the organization. In a mature organization, where all strategies are fully articulated, the task of portfolio management can easily be delegated to a team other than the upper management, albeit, managed by the team in precise accordance with the articulated wishes of upper management. Under typical circumstances, the project team is focused on the project, while the upper management is focused on the portfolio, and there is little carryover from one of these functions to the other.

Even if there is some overlap between the personnel who perform the project management and portfolio management functions, the focus of the activities of these two teams is distinctly different. In managing a project, the project team is concerned with the activities to complete a deliverable, and, therefore, there is a tactical tone to all activities, even though the team will place a secondary focus on the effectiveness of these activities in terms of cost and schedule. On the other end of this spectrum, during the portfolio management process, the portfolio team is concerned with the deliverables as they relate to organizational strategic direction. Likewise, the portfolio management team might place a secondary focus on the cost and duration of each deliverable.

Midstream project evaluation is as critical as the original selection, maybe more so because it will deal with project termination, which can be highly emotionally charged. Even if the project was fully aligned with organizational business objectives at the authorization stage, midstream evaluation should be viewed as formalized testing of that alignment. During midstream evaluations, the project vision will be revisited in order to verify that the project deliverable continues to be responsive to that particular vision.

Project-level data/information primarily relate to scope, quality, cost, schedule, and risk. When these data are rolled up to the program level, if in fact the project is part of a program and is not standalone, the program data will be compiled information for scope, cost, resource demand, delivery dates, and risks. The program-level information will be compared against budgets, constraints, and organizational priorities. The contents of a program-level report will provide the foundation for making modifications to the projects, not necessarily as a result of the progress of the project itself, but rather, as a result of the combined attributes of the projects in the light of the program imperatives. Further, the portfolio-level information will also deal with total costs, delivery dates, and scope of deliverables. The difference between the decision process of programs and portfolios is that the portfolio-level decisions will be heavily tempered by organizational strategic imperatives, whereas programs will be heavily tempered by the performance of the collective projects within the program.

The aggregation and rollup of data across portfolios are primarily focused on cost, cash flow demand, resource demand, milestones, and deliverables. Since the basic data for these project attributes exist in quantitative form, the summarization is usually a simple summation across time and/or across a portfolio. By contrast, attributes that relate to the project's business case and the impact of one project on the success of another project are usually qualitative and less defined. Enterprises that have difficulty quantifying the latter set of attributes are those that form committees and boards that debate the relative importance of these attributes, in lieu of quantifying them.

The team that is responsible for managing an individual project is primarily focused on managing things issues and people issues of projects and not necessarily enterprise issues. Things-related duties include management of cost, schedule, risk, quality, and scope. People-related duties include management of communications, conflict, staff motivation, and team morale. Enterprise-related duties include management of strategic alignment, return on investment, cash flow, and organizational change.

One of the goals of formalized management of a single project is that the expertise and wisdom of the experienced personnel in managing cost, schedule, and risk have been explicitly articulated, and formalized, for the benefit of the entire enterprise. In that vein, a formalized PPM approach has a similar foundation in that its goal is to make explicit what is implicit in project selection metrics, project selection processes, prioritization of projects, and assignment of resources to authorized projects.

Facilitating and promoting a formalized manage-by-project mentality is the underlying vision of the Enterprise Project Management Office (EPMO), and this vision can assure success for individual projects and their hosting portfolios. An increase in the involvement of the project management personnel in management-by-project activities is one of the attributes of a maturing organization. Improvements in competitive edge and competitive issues are the net result of PPM. The key is that managing projects should be done in an informed fashion and not in an ad-hoc manner. Then the project management professionals can show upper management and external clients that success is calculated by design and is highly repeatable. Finally, the increase in the use of virtual teams adds to the need for more effective procedures at the project level and at the enterprise level.

Several elements will have to be in place before an organization can claim that it conducts its activities on a management-by-projects basis. First and foremost, the organization must have a sophisticated project management

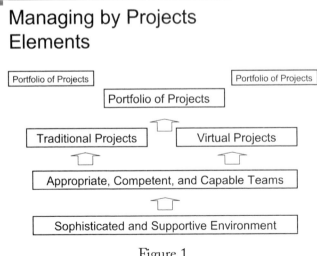

Figure 1

culture as evidenced by a project environment that is friendly to, and supportive of, projects (Figure 1).

With such a foundation, it will be possible to create and maintain competent and capable teams for the projects that carry out the missions of the organization. The competency of the team members must go beyond the management of project things, people, and technical specialty content. Although not everyone is suited to work on a virtual team, those who are in fact compatible with the virtual environment must be identified so that successful virtual teams can be formed when the occasions arise. The final stage of sophistication will be to relate all projects to one another and to the organization's funding structure. Such a collective view of projects will be achieved through the use of a methodical PPM system and through the use of very few portfolios, preferably, only one.

Depending on the maturity and sophistication of the organization, projects are viewed, handled, and managed either in isolation of each other or in aggregate. In a typical organization, projects are funded separately, reviewed separately, and probably never terminated for reasons other than excessive cost and duration overrun. In slightly mature organizations, projects are related to each other in a technical way and are treated together collectively as part of the management of the program. The next level of sophistication will be observed when the funding of projects is achieved through the use of a

Project Management Spectrum

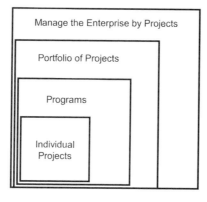

Manage the Enterprise by Projects

Portfolio of Projects

Programs

Individual Projects

Figure 2

single portfolio of projects, and thus, all of those projects are evaluated and reevaluated together. Finally, the ultimate level of sophistication is achieved when there are several portfolios that encompass all of the projects of the organization, and, better yet, when there is one all-inclusive portfolio that contains all of the projects (Figure 2).

The functions of a full-scale portfolio management system can be divided into two major categories: selecting projects for execution and managing those projects to a successful completion. The selection, prioritization, and affirmation of projects is a periodically repeating activity (Figure 3) in that a

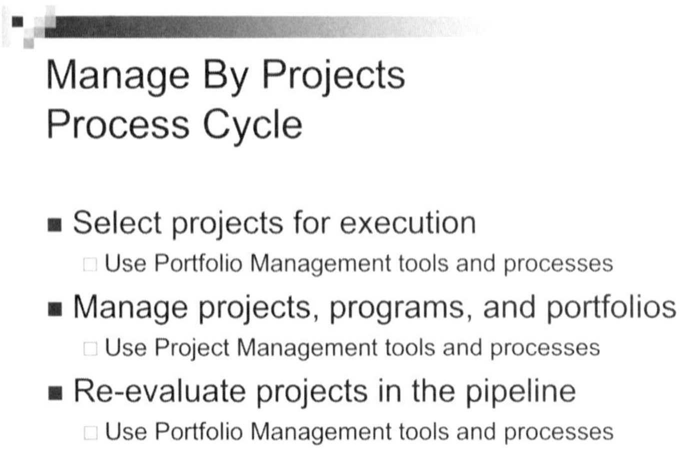

Manage By Projects Process Cycle

- Select projects for execution
  - Use Portfolio Management tools and processes
- Manage projects, programs, and portfolios
  - Use Project Management tools and processes
- Re-evaluate projects in the pipeline
  - Use Portfolio Management tools and processes

Figure 3

new project will be examined for authorization by the system, and that the wisdom of authorization will repeatedly be verified through midstream evaluation of that project. On the other hand, managing projects is a continuous activity for each project, the starting point of which will be when the project is first authorized. Naturally, project performance data will be continually generated, and periodically reported to the prioritization function. Hopefully, the project performance data are such that continuation of this project can be re-authorized during the next midstream evaluation.

Considering the overall cost of managing organizational projects, one can divide the costs into two cost components: implicit and explicit. If the organization has a large number of projects that are not contributing to the organization's strategic goals, or do not meet their stakeholders' desired expectations, there is an implicit wasted cost to the organization. By virtue of the fact that an organization incurs this wasted implicit cost, it is highly likely that there are no accounting structures in place to measure the magnitude of the implicit wasted cost. At the other end of the spectrum, there is a nominal, but quantifiable, explicit cost involved in establishing the PPM system. On balance, the explicit cost is lower than the implicit cost, as evidenced by improved profitability in organizations that implement a formalized project management system. (Figure 4)

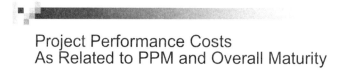

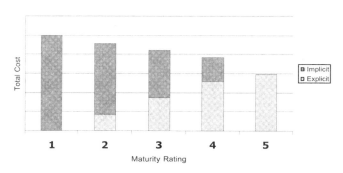

Figure 4

Although management of portfolios of projects and management of singular projects are components of a fully functioning EPMO, they tend to focus on two different aspects of project management. To select the projects for execution, one would use the PPM tools, while to manage those projects, one would use the single-project management tools. During the midstream portfolio reevaluation, one would use the PPM tools, and the cycle will continue. It is entirely possible that a typical organization might have a crude form of the portfolio management system, in which case the management of projects usually would depend on the team-focused functions of the EPMO. However, if a mature organization implements a portfolio management system, and, hopefully, a methodical portfolio management system, then the projects that are selected will primarily be managed using the enterprise-oriented functions of the EPMO (Figure 5). Project management maturity is, or should be, of utmost interest to those executives who have a purely business vantage point in their decisions and initiatives. A mature organization is apt to be more efficient, more innovative, and more profitable. Such an organization is likely to have high employee morale and an exceptionally high competitive edge (Figure 6).

The motivation for implementing PPM can be from the desire for improvements in operational efficiency, improvements in cost savings, and increased profits. Interestingly enough, an effective PPM system will result in all three, regardless of which motivation was the basis of implementation.

Managing a Portfolio of Projects

Select Projects	Conduct Portfolio Management
Manage Projects	Perform Project Management
Re-Evaluate Projects	Conduct Portfolio Management

	Immature organizations *use inefficient team-focused tools and techniques*
	Mature organizations *use sophisticated enterprise-oriented tools and techniques*

Figure 5

Maturity Implications

- Efficiency
- Innovations
- Morale
- Competitive edge
- Profits

Figure 6

There is no question that project success should always be celebrated and acknowledged. However, it would be unrealistic to treat project success as a matter of good luck. To the contrary, project success should be treated as a direct consequence of good project management practices. Such practices will inform the project managers and the upper management about the realistic status of current and past projects, by way of setting standards for future projects. Effective project management practices would also promote a clear articulation of the business cases that create the various projects. It is this formal articulation of the business cases of projects that becomes the guiding light for the prioritization of the projects within the portfolio. Finally, the incidents of good project management practices are concurrent with the desirable situations where only useful and relevant projects are funded. A methodical selection of projects will result in a reduction of the number of marginal projects in the pipeline. The marginality of projects could stem either from cost-schedule performance or from the value that the deliverable will impart to the organization (Figure 7).

Success By Design

- Formalized Project Management Results in:
  - ☐ Informed Management of Projects
  - ☐ Effective Management of Projects
  - ☐ Formalized Articulation of Project Business Case
  - ☐ Increased Favorable Competitive Edge
  - ☐ Planned Success, Not Accidental Success
  - ☐ Pursuit of Useful and Relevant Projects
  - ☐ Reduction of Marginal Projects
    - Marginal in Performance
    - Marginal in Utility

Figure 7

If an organization has a fully functional EPMO, then more than likely the organization has achieved the highest level of project management maturity, partly because of the facilitations that it would bring to managing projects and partly because of the infrastructure and organizational friendliness that the EPMO would demand for its full operation. At the other end of the spectrum, the first organizational attempt at project management sophistication is usually the establishment of a project office for a runaway project, and then for another runaway project, and then yet for another one. The repetition of this activity, because of its temporary nature, and lack of its incentive for organizational memory, will be significantly more costly and yet without any real long-term benefit.

Ideally, one would expect that the enterprise is fully successful in managing individual projects when the enterprise implements a system to manage the portfolio that contains those projects. On the other hand, there could be cases where the PPM system emerges first, thus prompting a consistent and formalized project management system within the enterprise. If the implementation of a PPM precedes the implementation of an EPMO within the enterprise, then the PPM will end up implementing portions of an EPMO within the organization, even if it might not be called an EPMO. The crucial point is that, ultimately, a successful PPM system and a project-friendly environment will go hand in hand in creating a suite of appropriate and successful projects.

Independent of whether PPM precedes an EPMO, or the other way around, a PPM system will contribute to an environment where project success is a well-defined concept, and where continuous improvement is the norm. PPM will facilitate a suite of relevant projects in an objective and methodical fashion, which in turn will promote effective communication and improved motivation for successful and efficient implementation of individual projects. The combination of strategically focused projects, and highly motivated teams to implement them, will go a long way toward achieving overall organizational goals.

Chapter Summary. A project portfolio management system is an essential part of an enlightened organization, although all organizations would benefit from some form of such a function. Project portfolio management involves a logical and formalized selection of projects and a methodical execution of these projects to their logical and successful conclusion.

An effective project portfolio management system process serves to identify, analyze, and quantify project value on a regular basis; to prioritize projects; and to identify which projects to initiate, reprioritize, or terminate. Specifically, it allows managers to answer questions such as:

• Which projects will best support the organization's business strategies and goals?
• Is a project or program providing the anticipated business results,
as demonstrated by portfolio metrics?
• Does each project in the portfolio have appropriate resources, including staff with the right skill sets?

The objective of PPM is to select and prioritize projects to deliver the highest value in accordance with the pre-established portfolio management business decisions and priority criteria. Priority should be based on both individual project benefits and overall impact to the organization. In addition, the resulting portfolio mix must not exceed the organization's resource capacity and capability.

Appendix 1

Project Portfolio Management Literature Review

The practice of managing a portfolio of projects was initially crafted after the concepts of financial portfolio management. However, gradually and continually, it has evolved into a separate entity, which deals with the specifics of a project management environment. This appendix summarizes the developmental highlights of this concept.

Historical Background of Portfolio Management

Portfolio theory was introduced by Harry Markowitz (1952) with his paper on "Portfolio Selection." Before this work, investors focused on assessing the risks and benefits of individual securities. Investment analysts identified securities that offered the most promising opportunities for gain with the least amount of risk and then constructed a portfolio from these securities. This approach resulted in a set of securities that involved, for example, the pharmaceutical industry or the automotive industry.

Markowitz instead suggested that investors focus on selecting portfolios based on their overall risk-reward characteristics, rather than only compiling portfolios from securities that had attractive risk-reward characteristics. Markowitz noted that if single-period returns for various securities were treated as random variables, they could be assigned expected values, standard deviations, and correlations. This led to the ability to calculate the expected return and volatility of any portfolio constructed with these securities.

He connected linear programming and investments, noting that the desired output is a higher return, while the cost to be minimized is the volatility of the return. To construct this model, the expected return of each potential component of the portfolio was required, along with determination of the expected volatility of each component's return, and the expected correlation of each component with every other component. To determine these returns, Markowitz suggested use of the observed values for past periods.

Markowitz's model identified the various components that will yield the best trade-offs between return and volatility for the portfolio. Certain portfolios would optimally balance risk and reward, which Markowitz called an "efficient frontier" of portfolios. The investor then should select a portfolio that lies on the "efficient frontier," as each portfolio would offer the maximum possible expected return for a given level of risk. This model laid the foundation for the development of portfolio theory, although Markowitz acknowledged that anticipating the future could be as much an art as a science.

Tobin (1958) expanded on Markowitz's work and added a risk-free asset to the analysis in order to leverage or de-leverage, as appropriate, portfolios on the "efficient frontier" leading to the concepts of a super-efficient portfolio and the capital market line. With leverage, portfolios on the capital market line could outperform portfolios on the "efficient frontier." Sharpe (1964) then prepared a capital asset pricing model that noted that all investors should hold the market portfolio, whether leveraged or de-leveraged, with positions on the risk-free asset.

However, even earlier, Bernoulli (1738), in an article about the St. Petersburg Paradox, stated that risk averse investors should diversify. Bernoulli explained that goods that are exposed to some small danger should be divided into several portions rather than grouping them all together as a single unit. Markowitz (1999) later noted that that Bernoulli's work was superseded by that of William Shakespeare in the Merchant of Venice, Act 1, Scene 1, in which Antonio said:

> ". . . I thank my fortune for it,
> My ventures are not in one bottom trusted,
> Nor to one place; nor is my whole estate
> Upon the fortune of this present year . . ."

Markowitz at this time pointed out though that while diversification would reduce risk, it still could not eliminate risk. He stated that an investor should maximize expected portfolio return, while minimizing portfolio variance of return. One stock might provide long-term growth, while another might generate short-term dividends. Some stocks should be part of the portfolio in order to insulate it from wide market fluctuations.

Markowitz's approach now is common among institutional portfolio managers to structure their portfolios and measure their performance and is used to manage the portfolios of ordinary investors. Its extension has led to increasingly refined theories of the effects of risk on valuation. The mathematics of portfolio theory are used extensively in financial risk management as financial portfolio managers concentrate their efforts on achieving the most optimal trade-offs between risk and return, taking into account the different levels of risk tolerance of different investors. The portfolio model, therefore, strives to obtain the maximum return with the minimum risk. Project and portfolio managers thus estimate expected returns, standard deviations, and correlations. The mean is the expected return of each potential project, and the variance or standard deviation measures the risk associated with the portfolio.

In 1990, Markowitz, along with Merton Miller and William Sharpe, shared a Nobel Prize for their work on a theory for portfolio selection. Portfolio theory provides a context to help understand the interactions of systematic risk and reward. It has helped to shape how institutional portfolios are managed and fostered the use of passive investment management techniques. It led to the use of portfolio management in numerous other areas, especially in project management, as more and more organizations move toward adopting a management-by-projects approach. This was pointed out by Cleland and King (1983) in which they stated that the increase in use of project management led to many projects that were outside of the organization's specific mission, that were unrelated to the organization's strategic direction, and also were ones with funding levels that were not commensurate relative to the organization's expected benefits.

Introduction of Portfolio Management to Projects

As noted by Essex (2005) in the late 1990s, portfolio management became popular for information technology projects, and several vendors released software that enabled managers to categorize projects within portfolios and share collective data. Other tools were introduced to assist in further identification of business goals and to evaluate the contributions of project portfolios to these goals. Project selection thus involves assessing individual projects as well as groups of projects and then determining which ones to implement so that the objectives of the organization can be achieved (Meredith and Mantel, 2006).

Further, in 2006, the Project Management Institute (PMI, 2006) issued a Portfolio Management Standard. The purpose of this stadard is to focus "on portfolio management as it relates the discipline of project and program management" (p. 3), and it applies to all types of organizations.

According to Meredith and Mantel (2006), models can be simple to understand or complex. If more reality is introduced, the model is more difficult to manipulate. In deciding upon a specific model, Souder (1973) suggests consideration of realism, capability, flexibility, ease of use, and cost. Meredith and Mantel (2006) add the ease of use of its computerization as an additional criterion for consideration.

Stage-Gate Model

One of the better known portfolio management models is the stage-gate model proposed by Cooper, Edgett, and Kleinschmidt (2001), in which the project is broken down into several review phases called stages. The milestone between two successive phases is called a gate. The key to this process is that the validity of the project is revisited at every milestone, hence the name stage gate. Probably the most valuable facet of this approach is the identification of the milestones at which the validity of the project needs to be affirmed for it to go forward. Naturally, the number and texture of project phases would be different in different industries, maybe even in different projects. Accordingly, the nature of the inter-phase tests, which will be conducted at the gates, would be industry specific and even project specific.

Cooper, Edgett, and Kleinschmidt (2001) explained that portfolio management is fundamental to successful product development and states that it is the "operationalization" of business strategy. Typically, it is not handled well and is a major business challenge. However, they note that product success requires portfolio management. The key is to maximize the value of the portfolio but also to ensure that the portfolio is balanced appropriately, there are the right number of projects in the portfolio, and the portfolio is strategically aligned. They note that no one model can realize all four of these goals so multiple methods tend to be used to select projects.

Cooper, Edgett, and Kleinschmidt (1998a) explained that early project selection methods were not sophisticated in the sense that they used quantitative techniques such as linear programming, non-linear programming, integer programming, and decision trees. They also did not consider many variables in the same model. Baker and Freeland (1975) noted that many of these early methods were basically ignored, and the decision-theory models, for instance, were rarely used. They added that while scoring models were more popular, the most prevalent method actually used was traditional capital budgeting. They stated that the trend was not to use decision models and instead to use decision information systems. Later, Liberatore and Titus (1983) stated that even though managers were familiar with mathematical programming models, they tended to avoid their actual use.

According to Cooper, Edgett, and Kleinschmidt (1998a), these early techniques further emphasized maximizing value rather than ensuring balancing or aligning the portfolio to the company's strategy. The models focused on financial projections of each project's commercial value. The financial models used net present value (NPV) and ranked the projects based on NPV divided by the key or constraining resource. They emphasized the monetary value of the project rather than its technical or strategic advantage. For example, projects could be ranked by dividing NPV by the remaining research and development costs to be spent on the project. Other approaches centered on decision-analysis techniques, the Program Evaluation Review Technique (PERT)/Critical Path Method (CPM), and Monte Carlo simulations.

Additionally, the models at that time were costly and difficult to use, unlike similar models available today. Schmidt and Freeland (1992) stated that perhaps the problem was a mismatch between the various modeling efforts and modeling needs. They felt that this was due to concentrating attention on modeling a problem focused on outcomes, rather than developing approaches to enable decision makers to gain insight into the decision-making processes.

Notwithstanding, given that these techniques did not deliver a definite solution to the problem of prioritizing projects on a massive scale, many mapping techniques have been used to help portfolio management personnel visualize and compare different aspects of the projects in the portfolio, using bubbles, circles, and a variety of labels for the projects groups. Classic tools include checklists, sorting or mapping models, and scoring models using financial or non-financial measures.

Mapping of Projects

As noted by Hussey (1998), portfolio analysis is an approach used in strategic planning to compare various business activities to one another in order to establish priorities and decide between winners and losers. Hussey noted that General Electric is credited with developing an approach that divided activities into strategic business units that corresponded to the life cycle of its products. These strategic business units, for example, were set up to be a composite of the product and a geographical area. For instance, a product may be more mature in certain areas, such as in developed companies, and less mature in newly established companies. As Hussey stated, this may then mean that there could be two strategic business units, instead of one, on a more traditional product grouping.

This approach initially was popularized by the Boston Consulting Group (BCG) in a paper titled "The Product Portfolio" (1970). BCG stated that "to be successful, a company should have a portfolio of products with different growth rates and different market shares." BCG distinguished between high-growth products that require cash inputs to grow, and low-growth products that should generate excess cash; both types of products were needed simultaneously. BCG titled products with high market share and slow growth as "cash cows" and products with low market share and slow growth as "pets" which are not necessary as they show evidence of failure to obtain a leadership position during a growth period or to get out and cut losses appropriately. Ultimately every product should be a cash generator, and a balanced portfolio is one which has stars with high share and high growth to assure the future, cash cows that are used to supply funds for future growth, and question marks, which are products to be converted into stars later with added funds.

The BCG approach led to many other techniques that have been used as ways to prioritize projects in a portfolio such as "must have, should have, nice to have" (Wysocki and McGarry, 2003). These tools are helpful in terms of visualizing the balance in the portfolio and can incorporate multiple criteria in a single diagram, but they do not enable ranking of projects within the portfolio (Dickinson, Thornton, and Graves, 2001).

The Q-Sort approach for projects is one method to consider. It is based on work done initially by Stephenson (1953) to help rank or prioritize valuable, complex, and partially overlapping models. Its purpose is to enable researchers to examine subjective perceptions of individuals on various topics. When it is used, participants in the process receive a sheet with specific sorting instructions and an answer sheet for rank ordering. A correlation matrix of the participants is prepared, factor analysis is used, and a factor loading or correlation coefficient is prepared to show how the individual perceptions are similar or dissimilar to the composite factor array (Brown, 2004). It therefore can be used to measure the extent and nature of agreement on projects to be part of a portfolio and their ranking within the portfolio.

In a typical application of Q-Sort to PPM, projects are divided into two groups: high priority and low priority. These projects are further decomposed into three groups: high priority, medium priority, and low priority. They are decomposed again into: highest priority, high priority, medium priority, low priority, and lowest priority (Wysocki and McGarry, 2003). Another approach (Helin and Souder, 1974) is to divide the projects into three groups—good, fair, and poor—according to relative merits. If a group has more than eight projects in it, it is then subdivided according to fair-plus and fair-minus. Then, projects in each category are ordered from highest to lowest.

Other examples of such depictions are risk-reward diagrams that use four quadrants for the four combinations of high-low risk and reward. In risk-reward diagrams, the cost of a project is depicted by the size of the circle (Kendall and Rollins, Wysocki and McGarry, and Frame). Additionally, the pattern in the circles could represent one or two attributes of the project, and different icons can be used to depict strategic fit of the project. The circles can be replaced by ellipses if the exact values are not known and if a range estimate only is available for one of the two variables. Another plot is one that can be used where business strength and market opportunity are plotted against each other, with projects plotted with their cost or other attributes shown by icons or patterns.

A "Bubble Diagram" is another approach that can be prepared. Its purpose is to show, through color coding, shapes, and other attributes, multiple variables. It displays key parameters required to successfully balance a project portfolio (Milosevic, 2003). The x and y axes show the key dimensions or parameters. Then, adding the bubble to the diagram shows how the project positions itself according to the two dimensions. Around the diagram, Milosevic states are bubbles, visualized as projects. One is then able to see projects in favorable quadrants of the diagram, and the diagram can assist managers in determining how best to balance the portfolio.

However, many executives find these images far too complicated, and as a result, this approach often is not considered too valuable (Kendall and Rollins, 2003). Cooper, Edgett, and Kleinschmidt (2001) further explain that these bubble diagrams, along with pie charts that show a breakdown of product types by various categories, are not decision models per se but instead are ones appropriate for "information display" (p. 3) in that they show the current portfolio and how resources are allocated. They are helpful since they provide a useful way to determine how resources should be allocated. Milosevic (2003) explains that it is difficult for a single chart to characterize a portfolio completely. Multiple charts may be required starting at the hierarchy of the company for the most strategic projects and then cascading downward to other organizational levels. With a large number of bubble diagrams, though, information overload may result, and balancing projects within the portfolios may increase in complexity.

Frame (2003) suggests the use of gap analysis as a technique to visualize the practical budget options available in specific portfolios. It uses both exploratory and normative forecasting. In this approach, normative forecasting addresses the future and what it will take to get there, while exploratory forecasting focuses on extrapolating from past experience into the future. Frame notes that exploratory forecasting is helpful in preparing estimates of future budget demands of projects that are currently in the portfolio.

Another approach (Groenveld, 1997) uses a precedence diagram to map the interdependencies between projects and their potential economic benefit. Its purpose is to relate research technologies to potential products and final markets. In this technique, product-technology roadmaps are graphed on a horizontal time scale against potential economic benefit. Links between the projects and the enterprise strategy are displayed, but the approach does not consider the balance of the portfolio nor does it maximize its financial return.

Scoring Models

Scoring models provide decision makers with information to rank proposed projects and select projects to pursue based on criteria and resource availability. A scoring model typically consists of four basic components:

1. Categories of criteria to determine the model type
2. Range of values for the criteria
3. Measurement and description for each value within the range
4. Importance or weight of the criteria

The ranking involves identifying appropriate criteria or drivers that will allow for differentiation between the projects. Each criterion is associated with a range of values to identify where the project falls within the criterion. This value is usually on a numeric scale with the highest value positioning the project higher in the priority list, and the lowest value positioning the project lower on the scale. Along with values associated to each criterion, a weight will also be assigned to position the criterion with the appropriate importance. While these models potentially are easy to use, the criterion ranking is not precise. As a result, the outcome should be considered a guide-line, recognizing that people make decisions, not models. Further, time is required to determine the criteria, the weights, and the values as well as to obtain buy-in throughout the organization. The criteria used must be objective so that people cannot "skew the model to select pet projects" (Armstrong, 2004).

Cooper, Edgett, and Kleinschmidt (2001) describe this approach as one in which the decision makers rate projects to determine a Project Attractiveness Score based on a number of questions, typically on a 1-5 or 0-10 scale. The Project Attractiveness Score must clear a minimum hurdle. The score then becomes a proxy for the "value of the project" (p. 4) but includes strategic, leverage, and other considerations, rather than solely financial measures. These factors are scored for each project during gate review meetings. Factors may include items such as the strategic attractiveness, product/competitive advantage, market attractiveness, synergies in terms of leveraging core competencies, technical feasibility, and risk versus return. Projects are rank ordered until there are no resources remaining.

Martino (2003) suggests inclusion of criteria such as cost, the probability of technical success, the probability of market success, payoff, market size, market share, the availability of resources, the degree of organizational commitment, the project's strategic position, the degree of competition, constraints associated with the regulatory environment, and any policy considerations of the company. He suggests that criteria be classified in terms of overriding criteria, tradable criteria, and optional criteria. Next, the value and the importance of the criteria are determined, and measures for the criteria are identified to see which criteria can be measured objectively and which ones require judgment. Martino notes, though, that these scoring models are a "one-level" (p. 32) process, such that if one or more of the criteria are comprised of sub-criteria that are combined to obtain the value for a factor, any combination must be done outside of the specific model.

Use of a Strategic Alignment Model with Weighted Criteria according to Wysocki and McGarry (2003) is one scoring model to consider. The purpose of this approach is to align projects in terms of the direction the organization has decided to follow based on those items that are considered to be the most important. In this method, the starting point is the value or mission statement of the organization. It is in turn broken down into specific goals, and then each goal is broken down further into objectives. Each objective then is weighted with a number between 0 and 1, such that all of the objectives' weights then sum to 1, and to show the importance of each objective in comparison with the other objectives. The next step is to assign a budget to each objective. Then, the projects proposed for the portfolio, and their budgets, are ranked according to each of the objectives, as projects often will support more than one objective. The project's budget next is broken down in terms of the specific amount of the budget that will support each associated objective with weights also assigned to show the importance of the project to the objective. The sum of the weights is 1. Then, a priority order for the various projects in the portfolio is determined by multiplying the objective weight by the project weight and adding the numbers. Based on the project's score, projects are rank ordered to show the ones that should be funded.

Raz (1997) developed an iterative rating project as another alternative to a scoring model. In it he begins with a set of attributes to use to rank projects. His next step is to remove attributes that do not differentiate between alternatives and all projects that are dominated by others. If a choice can be made, the process stops, otherwise it is repeated.

Meredith and Mantel (2006) suggest the use of a weighted scoring model since this type of model enables multiple objectives of the organization to be reflected in the decisions concerning those projects to support and those to terminate. They also note that these models can be adapted based on changes and do not include a bias toward short-term gains as can be the case in profitability models. They also feel that these models are straightforward, however, their use forces decision makers to make difficult choices. Additionally, these models can be simulated, as the weights and scores are typically estimates. One approach they describe is a constrained weighted factor scoring model to add additional criteria as constraints, rather than weighted factors. Such an approach can avoid the temptation to include marginal criteria. Constraints then represent project characteristics that must be present or absent for the project to be successful.

The U.S. Government Accountability Office (GAO) notes the importance of defining the scoring elements, for example, if a 1 to 5 Likert type scale is to be used, what is represented by a 1 versus a 5? Uniform definitions will promote objectivity in the scoring process so there are fewer inconsistencies as portfolio management is implemented throughout the organization. The same criteria to rank and compare projects should be used in the same way for implementation success. The GAO recommends a minimum set of criteria for use enterprise-wide, with other criteria used at different levels of the organization. The GAO further suggests that the process be designed so people have incentives to comply with it, and also so "gamesmanship" is discouraged. Explicit consequences for noncompliance should be in place, especially early in the implementation process.

A checklist is a variation of a scoring model. While it still uses multiple criteria in multiple categories, each criterion is answered with a yes or no, and a single no can eliminate the project from further consideration. With the use of a checklist, projects also are not ranked or balanced in the portfolio (Cooper, Edgett, and Kleinschmidt, 1998b).

The Analytical Hierarchy Process

In the 1970s, Thomas Saaty (1980) developed the Analytical Hierarchy Process (AHP) to set priorities and make the best decision using both qualitative and quantitative approaches. The AHP reduces complex decisions to a series of one-on-one comparisons and then synthesizes the results. It uses subjective, pair-wise comparisons. This enables determination of numeric weights of decision criteria and criteria scores for alternatives. Decision makers then can select the best alternative based on the value measured by a hierarchy of sub-objectives or attributes. It expands on the traditional scoring methods as it includes means to incorporate sub-criteria. As Martino (2003) explains, the approach provides an opportunity to seek cause-effect explanations between goals, criteria, sub-criteria, and candidate projects. When the hierarchical structure is established, it can weight the criteria and sub-criteria to determine a composite score for each project at each level, as well as an overall score. The overall score shows the merit of the project.

Martino notes that the purpose of the AHP was not to assist in ranking projects but instead was developed to support decision making regardless of the specific nature of the decision. It is an approach that can be used for any type of decision in which multiple alternatives are available. The first step is to structure the decision process in a hierarchy. The goal is shown at the top of the hierarchy. The next level shows the criteria that are relevant for the goal followed by the various alternatives to be evaluated. Then, alternatives are compared to the criteria. Finally, comparisons are synthesized, and results are summarized to obtain the overall priority of the alternative.

The AHP helps to reduce risk through the selection of the best alternative. It is used frequently for large, complex projects, new project selection, and stage-gate reviews on existing projects. However, Martino cautions that decision makers can assign different levels of importance to a particular criterion, and the approach becomes complex as the number of criteria increases. In 1983, Saaty, along with Ernest Forman, co-founded Expert Choice, a company with a specialized software tool using AHP (www.expertchoice.com). Other automated approaches also are available, as well as a number of variations of the approach.

Dependency Matrix and Optimization Model

Addressing some of the limitations of the above approaches, Dickinson, Thornton, and Graves (2001) developed the Dependency Matrix and Optimization Model tools. The Dependency Matrix is a scalable, flexible method used to document and quantify the interdependencies between project portfolios. After the matrix is prepared, the next step is to determine the amount of the project revenue that is attributable to a single project, as well as the amount that is attributable to its interdependencies with other projects in the portfolio by determining a minimum benefit level, or the revenue if the project was funded, regardless of funding for other dependent projects. The matrix also can be used to evaluate a portfolio across either a single period or multiple periods based on the projects that are funded. The matrix is updated as new projects are added to the portfolio, deleted from it, or combined with other projects.

Dickinson, Thornton, and Graves' (2001) Optimization Model uses data from the Dependency Matrix, along with estimated financial performance, to calculate total portfolio performance through a non-linear, integer program. Its purpose is to maximize the ultimate financial return, considering portfolio balance and budget constraints. The model then is used to evaluate different mixes of projects within the portfolio.

Real Options Approach

Martino (2003) suggests consideration of the Real Options Approach as a method of project selection that presents a way to select projects that is analogous to selecting financial options. He believes this approach is helpful for a project that is too large to be treated as overhead but is not ready to be considered as a capital investment. If the project is one in which there are a wide range of possible payoffs, it then is a candidate project for future investments. Investing in this approach is similar to selecting an opportunity to make a further investment if the investment is one that is profitable. Risks must be identified for the project, and methods to offset these risks must be determined. There may be options that the organization might take to reduce each of the specific risks, which Martino states are shadow options. This forces project professionals to confront risks. The next step is to determine different methods to structure the project. During this analysis, each method considers different combinations of the shadow options that have been identified. Then, the combination of the options that results in the most favorable option is determined, and the shadow options are converted into real options. A key advantage of this approach, according to Martino, is that it can translate "real project phenomena into visualizable effects" (p. 62). Disadvantages include the time, effort, and expense that are needed to implement the approach. It serves to determine when an attractive project is perhaps too risky to pursue.

Cooper, Edgett, and Kleinschmidt (2001) suggest the Expected Commercial Value approach to approximate real options theory for use with higher-risk projects. This approach uses decision-tree analysis and breaks the project into specific stages. Then, possible outcomes are defined along with the probabilities each one will occur, such as the probability of technical and commercial success. The resulting Expected Commercial Value is then divided by a constraining resource, and projects are rank ordered.

Agile Portfolio Management

Agile portfolio management is another approach to consider. According to Grant Thornton (2004), its purpose is to select projects that drive business goals and then invest in the resources required to execute them. In this approach, the portfolio management process is de-coupled from the business planning and budgeting cycle. It is based first on an accurate measurement of project options and alignment with business strategy, known as a valuation process. This is done by aggregating new project ideas as well as conducting an inventory of existing projects. A single channel is used with an appropriate valuation model and discount rate based on the risk level of the project and the staff expertise. The next step is to determine the business operating plan and the capabilities and processes that need to be in place so that the forecasted value can be realized. Grant Thornton points out that often intangible benefits and costs are not included, such as training costs, in project valuation. If a project is positively valued, then its strategic orientation is determined and is shown across two dimensions—the type of project and the time to payoff. They suggest four categories: strategic, utility, venture, and future utility.

Only valuable projects should be prioritized. This is done during a process in which project schedules are optimized according to value, priority, strategic orientation, and interdependencies. During this process a systems scenario analysis is performed to test assumptions made in the valuation process, and projects are rank ordered in terms of their alignment to strategic performance targets. Projects are prioritized, scheduled, and funded, with a prioritization decision involving whether the project should receive more resources than average, less funding than desired although it is considered to be a valuable project, minimal funding as the project is being phased out and shares few interdependencies with other projects, or whether the project is at the end of the life cycle and should be discontinued. Resources are allocated based on capacity and skills.

Chin (2004) further explains that with the agile approach, since resources are limited, the rapid change afforded through agile project management requires that resources can also be shifted efficiently and quickly between projects. The agile environment is characterized by more aggressive project schedules that often give the team little time to adjust and react to change. This is particularly the case when a new project is approved. Resources must be continually reallocated in an effective manner so that old projects are not dropped or postponed when a new project is approved. The impact of resource allocation on the overall business objectives must be determined. Grant Thornton (2004) further notes that training and recruiting plans are tied to the portfolio. People are incentivized to align their goals according to the needs of the portfolio, and the incentive system is a flexible one.

A Governance Board communicates prioritization decisions, the Enterprise Project Management Office (EPMO) manages delivery and monitors results, and the prioritization process is reassessed. The portfolio specifically is evaluated for risks and opportunities, testing assumptions about payoffs and dependencies in the valuation phase, and eliminating barriers. The goal is to avoid major changes to the portfolio and instead to make incremental, decisive changes as the dynamics of the organization and its environment change.

Unbalanced Portfolio Concerns

As noted by Dickinson, Thornton, and Graves (2001, p. 10), in a quote by W. Edwards Deming, "All models are wrong. Some models are useful." Regardless of the approach that is used, an unbalanced portfolio can result. As defined by Kendall and Rollins (2003), such a situation is noted by the following six examples of portfolio categories:

1. Too much on the supply side, not enough on the market side
2. Too much development, not enough research
3. Too much short term, not enough long term
4. Not reflective of the organization's most important assets
5. Not reflective of the organization's strategic resource value
6. Not reflective of major product revenue opportunities, risks, etc.

Project Portfolio Management Process

The Project Management Institute in its *A Guide to the Project Management Body of Knowledge,* Third Edition (PMBOK® Guide) defines a process as "a set of interrelated actions and activities that are performed to achieve a pre-specified set of products, results, or services" (p. 38). PMI separates processes into two categories: project management processes, which are common to most projects and serve to initiate, plan, execute, monitor and control, and close the project, and product-oriented processes, which involve the specification and creation of the product of the process. The Association of Project Management (APM) defines a process as "a set of interrelated resources and activities which transform inputs into outputs" (www.apm.org.uk).

Knutson (2001) states that the purpose of the PPM process is to provide a way to evaluate consistently and objectively each proposed project that is vying for a limited pool of resources. She presents a generic portfolio management process model, which consists of the five following stages: solicitation (to ensure the potential project that is being evaluated has a credible strategy that supports the organization's goals and strategy and includes the project's business case); selection (where the relative value of the project and its link to organizational strategy is assessed); prioritization (where a scoring system is used to determine the priority of the project in light of other projects); registration (where the project is now part of the ongoing projects in the organization); and resource allocation (where resources are allocated to the project depending on availability).

Crawford, Hobbs, and Turner (2005, p. 15), state that "The grouping of projects into categories is an essential step in the project portfolio management process." They note, however, that this categorization is different from that focused on project management, as it is based on selecting projects, aligning them with strategy, allocating resources, and balancing the portfolio. All are designed to maximize value to the organization through executive management visibility into the process.

Kendall and Rollins (2003) suggest six components in terms of a process to follow for project portfolio management:

1. Determine a viable mix of projects that can meet the organization's goals.
2. Balance the portfolio in terms of specific categories of projects.
3. Plan and execute these projects.
4. Analyze the performance of the projects in the portfolio to see if improvements are warranted.
5. Evaluate new opportunities against the projects in the portfolio and against other potential opportunities. This evaluation considers the capacity available in the organization to execute both the potential projects and the ongoing projects.
6. Provide decision makers with the needed information and recommendations.

Cable et al (2004) built on the Treemap Concept developed at the University of Maryland Human-Computer Interaction Laboratory in 1992, along with earned value, and applied it to PPM. This is a "space-filling visualization method for representing historical information" (p. 6). They presented an example of a project portfolio with 41 projects grouped by the phase of the project life cycle. Next, they calculated the Cost Performance Index, Schedule Performance Index, and Critical Ratio for each project. Then, visual maps were provided to show projects that only fell within a particular range. Through this approach, users can group projects according to specific requirements through a hierarchy and then examine the overall portfolio information through various filtering mechanisms. It further provides both project reports as well as portfolio performance changes over time.

As suggested by Varghese (2004), "A good process will tell what a good manager and staff would do anyway" (p. 13), and processes have always guided actions and determined business results. However, he states that "All processes are not created equally." Processes must be targeted to increase their ability to create or enable value. Varghese suggests that to target processes one must answer three questions: (1) What are the processes? (2) Which processes are the most important to the organization?, and (3) How well are these processes performing? Following Varghese's comments, the PPM process should be established to ensure that meaningful results are realized.

Portfolio Governance Review Boards

Rubin (as quoted in Datz, 2003) notes that "Portfolio management without governance is an empty concept." He further states that if companies have a weak governance structure, a portfolio management process can help them improve their governance structure. However, it also is important to recognize the purpose of governance. As stated in *CIO Magazine*, September 15, 2002, it is the structure to help make the decisions, not the decisions that are made, which is the purpose of management. Governance consists of the decision-making mechanisms such as committees and review boards, policies and procedures, and the level of authority assigned to these boards. The Organization for Economic Co-operation and Development (2004) explained that "Corporate governance also provides the structure through which the objectives of the company are set and the means of attaining those objectives and monitoring performance are determined." Meredith and Mantel (2006) explain that the purpose of governance is to "establish and articulate a strategic direction for those projects spanning internal or external boundaries of the organization" (p. 79). Additionally, it is responsible to allocate funds to those projects that are to be supported and to control the allocation of resources to those projects.

Ideally, a Governance or Review Board should have broad representation at the highest level of the organization, with participation by the executive decision makers. Additionally, Meredith and Mantel (2006) suggest that other members be the head of the EPMO, project managers of major projects, relevant general or functional managers, people who can identify the key opportunities and risks that face the organization as well as anyone who may wish to derail the portfolio management process at a later time. Establishing the Board can help to ensure the success of portfolio management in the organization.

Kendall and Rollins (2003) suggest that the Governance Board should set the direction for the portfolio and decide which projects should be approved, denied, activated, deactivated, terminated, require additional analysis, or require resource reallocation. The Board also serves to communicate decisions based on a communications plan. At its first meeting, the Board should set priorities in terms of active and proposed projects. Before each meeting, the Portfolio Manager submits status information to the Board. This, in turn, is noted by the Association for Project Management (2005, p. 4), which states that the purpose is to ensure that the organization's "Project portfolio is aligned to the organization's objectives, is delivered efficiently and is sustainable." The Governance or Review Board serves as a forum to discuss different issues and perspectives and to help build collaboration throughout the organization.

McFarland (2005) states that it is difficult in many organizations for the portfolio approach to rise to the top as different governance approaches may be needed. Some organizations may need more specialized governance by boards of directors, others may not. It is therefore imperative to determine the appropriate level of governance for the organization and to determine the number of governance review boards to establish in the organization. Ideally, a high-level, executive portfolio review board with an effective communications management plan and a dedicated portfolio manager is all that is required. However, there is a tendency to establish multiple review boards at various levels. Such an approach can become overly bureaucratic and can result in a decrease in creativity, innovation, and flexibility.

Also, it is necessary to determine how often the Governance Board should meet. Kendall and Rollins (2003) recommend that it meet once a month or more frequently if the organization's environment is one that is more fluid or in which the organization's customers are driving the demand for projects. They further suggest that quarterly meetings may not be frequent enough because of change that is so characteristic of today's projects.

The GAO, however, recommends that each project should be reviewed at key milestones in its life cycle with the review schedule established when the initial funding decision is made. It states that when the review is held, the context in which the program that the project supports should be considered. The GAO emphasizes the importance of continually assessing whether the program continues to make a contribution to the organization. The focus of the reviews should be on ensuring that benefits are being realized, risks are managed, and that the programs are contributing to strategic objectives.

Culture Change

Portfolio management is a culture change for organizations, especially for those organizations that allocate resources functionally and thus will now allocate resources across the enterprise. McFarland (2005) states that, "Changing the allocation rules can create a zero sum game in which there are clear winners and losers, something that may create more internal pain than people are willing to deal with." It could even be too great a transition unless a centralized process is in place to prioritize and manage the work through an EPMO. Otherwise, a significant change will be required. Communications, consensus-building, training, and the development of new policies, procedures, and practices will be required. People throughout the organization must be committed to the portfolio management process for its success.

2. The Enterprise Project Management Office: A Facilitator of Portfolio Management Success

Repeatable and predictable success of projects depends on formalized and standardized project management procedures and policies. In turn, policies, procedures, and tools can best be provided through an organizational focal point for project management. Equally important, there is a need for an atmosphere of facilitation and friendliness in the organization toward projects. A friendly environment can be attributed to the existence of facilitative features such as the methodologies, processes, procedures, controls, tools, people, and training. Other features of a friendly organization include all necessary components required to integrate projects into a portfolio, manage the portfolio, monitor the performance of projects, and create deliverables that meet an organization's business objectives successfully.

In order to meet the pressures of having successful projects, organizations are increasingly establishing Project Offices (PO), Project or Program Management Offices (PMO), or Enterprise Project Management Offices (EPMO). A PO is usually focused on the success of just one project. A PMO is usually commissioned to provide assistance for the success of only one division or organizational unit. An EPMO has the overarching mission of facilitating the success of all of the projects throughout the organization.

The benefits of an EPMO are somewhat subtle but significant. A fully functional EPMO would provide tools, techniques, and principles to the project team for project cost, schedule, scope, and quality. Additionally, the EPMO would provide tools and techniques to the portfolio team for project prioritization, midstream evaluation, and strategic alignment. The tools and techniques developed and maintained by the EPMO should provide schemas to deal with the seemingly nondescript areas of stakeholder satisfaction, team attitude, and team behavior. To serve the ongoing success of organizational projects, and to highlight the benefits of formalized project management, the EPMO must maintain a clearinghouse for project management best practices. These best practices would set the stage for successful management of projects on a regular basis.

The EPMO could be a recognized unit of a sector, department, or agency in order to facilitate its success in handling multiple projects, multiple resources, multiple locations, and key stakeholders. It is possible that to serve the immediate needs of some projects, the EPMO/PMO/PO could provide the structure, systems, and staff assistance for project managers to deal with difficult situations. Thus, depending on the maturity of the enterprise, the EPMO/PMO/PO will provide assistance in a wide range of areas from those that are highly reactive to fully proactive.

The existence of project portfolio management (PPM) and/or an EPMO would serve as an indication that the organization has a certain amount of commitment to project management maturity. The practical indications of organizational project management maturity are that projects are clearly linked to business strategy, there are consistent processes for projects and for portfolios, these processes are closely practiced, there is success in each and every aspect of all projects, and duties of all project management personnel are clearly defined.

Portfolio management, formalized project selection, formalized articulation of vision, and management by projects are all components of a sophisticated and enlightened organization. There is a very close relationship between the concept of managing by projects, the PPM process, the EPMO, and the concept of managing multiple projects from a single resource pool. For the purposes of this book, PPM will be used to collectively refer to the portfolio-related features of all three of these concepts.

2.1 Enterprise Project Management Office Functions

The entire spectrum of the functions of the EPMO includes two major categories: team-focused functions and enterprise-oriented functions. These two categories can also be described as those that yield short-term results, and those that yield long-term benefits. Figure 1 shows the collective description for all of the components of team-focused function groups and enterprise-oriented function groups. The comparison between the team-focused and enterprise-oriented categories of functions can be demonstrated by the following anecdotal distinction: the team-focused functions are those with which the EPMO does the project management work for the project management teams, whereas the enterprise-oriented functions are those with which the EPMO helps the project management team do the work themselves, efficiently and methodically. Depending on the circumstances, and on the maturity of the organization, the above-mentioned teams could be those that handle the projects, programs, or portfolios of the organization.

Functions of an EPMO

- Team-Focused Functions
    - Transient Mode
    - Day to day
    - Mission oriented
    - Short range
    - Local
    - Reactive
    - Do it for them
    - Crisis and firefighting
    - Tactical
- Enterprise-Oriented Functions
    - Stable and sophisticated
    - Long range
    - Global
    - Proactive
    - Help them do it themselves
    - Efficient
    - Strategic

Figure 1

The team-focused category can be described as transient mode, primarily because the organization will hopefully be developing plans to use these functions less and less as time passes. This set of functions is most appropriate for day-to-day activities. These functions tend to be highly localized, mission-oriented, short-range, and reactive. In many ways, the team-focused set of EPMO functions includes functions that are time-critical, and, therefore, they are akin to crisis management and firefighting. Depending on the maturity of the organization, the team-focused category might deal with individual projects, programs consisting of projects, or portfolios of projects (Figure 2). The team-focused functions of the EPMO include augmenting, mentoring, and consulting.

By comparison, the enterprise-oriented functions can be described as the stable, sophisticated, and efficient mode of operation. These functions are global, proactive, and mostly appropriate for long-range objectives. Ideally, the enterprise-oriented functions should be the only functions in force when the organization has reached the highest level of the maturity scale. The enterprise-oriented category of the EPMO functions includes training, clearing housing, providing best practices, and promoting the project management culture.

EPMO Functions

- **Team-Focused Functions**
  - Augment Portfolio/Project Management Team
  - Consult Individual Team Members
  - Mentor Individual Team Members
- **Enterprise-Oriented Functions**
  - Practice Formalized Portfolio/Project Management
  - Provide a Clearinghouse of Historical Data
  - Train Project Personnel and Functional Management
  - Promote a Project Management Culture

Figure 2

2.1.1 Team-Focused Functions

The team-focused set of functions includes those functions that EPMO staff might perform in order to provide assistance to teams who are responsible for individual projects, programs, or portfolios. Managing projects involves managing cost, schedule, and scope for an individual project. Managing programs involves managing cost, schedule, and scope in a multi-project environment and with a unified resource pool. Managing portfolios involves the development of a project prioritization model; use, maintenance, and enhancement of the prioritization model; and facilitating the conduct of the periodic project review process.

The team-focused functions of the EPMO are intended to have an immediate short-term impact on the project, program, or portfolio. In immature organizations, more often than not, team-focused functions are the only ones that are available to the organizational managers. These assistive and facilitative functions are provided through an abbreviated form of the EPMO, which is sometimes called the Project Office. Just the mere fact that the organization sets team-focused goals will give rise to the conclusion that the organization is not very mature. However, the fact cannot be over-stated that the overall cost of providing such short-term facilitation of success is far more than providing proactive, long-term solutions. Thus, the use of these functions should be regarded as a temporary measure and not as a routine operational norm.

When the collective resource demand for project management activities of several projects exceeds the availability of fully competent team members, the most efficient way to improve the likelihood of project success is to enlist the augmenting, mentoring, and consulting services of the EPMO's staff for the benefit of the less skilled team members. It is entirely likely that the team members are experts in the core business of the organization, although their project management skills would need to be enhanced. One would hope that the shortcomings in the technical area of expertise of the team members will be remedied by organizational centers of excellence dedicated to those technical specialties.

Augment. Augmentation is the process by which the EPMO serves in a fashion somewhat similar to a "temporary" agency in that it provides personnel of various skills to the team in order to fill any shortfalls that might exist within the team. Under this arrangement, the EPMO personnel simply provide a continuously available pool of additional resource hours for the team. Depending on the overall maturity of the organization, these teams can be engaged in managing projects, programs, or portfolios. If some of the enterprise-oriented functions of the EPMO exist in the organization, then these temporary project staff members will also serve as a conduit for best practices and company policies into the project. More than likely, the EPMO member who is on loan to the project team would assist with planning the project, developing project documents, monitoring the project progress, and developing remedies for those situations that involve cost overruns, schedule delays, or deliverable defects. This staff member could also support the team in its identification of risks, in its preparation of a risk management plan, and in developing risk responses. If the organization has implemented a portfolio management process, the EPMO temporary staff members on loan to the project team could work with the team to help the team prepare and submit prioritization reports, portfolio progress reports, and collective project reports.

Mentor. Mentoring occurs when the team has the right number of staff members, but the team members do not possess the appropriate project management competency in order to carry out their respective duties. In such a circumstance, the EPMO assigns a seasoned professional to assist, and work with, those team members that have shortfalls in their competencies. The mentor will work side by side with the team member for as long and as often as necessary until such time that the team member and/or the project manager feels comfortable that the team member can perform his or her functions without direct intervention by the EPMO staff member. A subtle and graceful means of phasing out the mentoring arrangement is to convert it to a consulting arrangement, where team empowerment is increased, while the EPMO involvement is decreased.

Consult. Consulting is the mode of assistance of choice when the team members feel comfortable performing most of their assigned duties, although they would like the comfort of validating the correctness of analysis, and the viability of assumptions, with a seasoned professional. Another mode of consultancy would be where the EPMO staff members periodically evaluate the work of team members through a shadowing work arrangement. Again, one would hope that, as the team members become more competent and as the team's comfort level is elevated, the consultancy incidents will be minimized.

2.1.2 Enterprise-Oriented Functions

In mature organizations, the EPMO is the focal point for improvement and enhancement in project management through the implementation of the enterprise-oriented functions. Enterprise-oriented functions are intended to bolster the overall capability of the organization for long-range benefits. The enterprise functions will provide the long-term stability and backbone for the project management success. This mission is met by establishing, and maintaining, a project historical database, by developing and disseminating project management best practices, by providing training in all project management knowledge areas, and by providing visibility for the value of project management to the organization.

It is crucial to develop organizational goals for the improvements in overall project management competence and then to compare the attained progress to the planned objectives. Essential in this process is the development of strategies for data collection, data refinement, data analysis, and reporting of the project performance results. Ultimately, the EPMO can and should establish measurable objectives for continuous improvement of enterprise project management sophistication.

The EPMO serves as a facilitator, an enabler, and an advocate for improved performance across all projects in the organization. The EPMO should maintain an extensive yet orderly archive of project performance data, together with an evolving list of lessons learned for all aspects of project management. The next natural step is to integrate and disseminate these best practices into the enterprise project management policies. Then, each project, each program, and each cycle of portfolio review should be considered as an opportunity for improvement in overall project management processes. The enterprise-oriented functions are to promote, archive, practice, and train.

Promote. Since the EPMO is the focal point for project management enhancement, the EPMO should continually maintain a support base with the senior executives and inform the entire organization of the project management success stories. The EPMO must routinely brief upper management on project management principles and on new developments in the profession. In order to integrate project management into the broader business context, the EPMO should publicize positive and successful project results and progress toward achieving organizational project management competency goals. Finally, the EPMO is the natural source for preparation and distribution of newsletters concerning project management in the organization and for the establishment of a portal to share lessons learned and new approaches in project management and to keep everyone apprised of project management successes in single projects, programs, and portfolios.

Archive. One of the more visible functions of an EPMO is recording and compiling the historical data for projects, programs, and portfolios. For best results, a standard data repository format must be used by all organizational teams. Therefore, the fundamental task of this function is that the EPMO must develop a standard approach to collecting multiple project data for programs and portfolios. Project documents on initial plans, change orders, and methods of change control are required as the project baseline information for progress data collection. Portfolio-related data will include details of the prioritization models such as the structure of the model, list of strategic indices, list of financial indices, and a list of project performance indices. With that backdrop, the EPMO should maintain project archives containing performance data spanning the entire project life cycle. Other data that must be derived from the project progress information include the productivity of various specialties in crafting, developing, and assembling project modules. The historical and performance data must be collected, refined, and archived. The data, and/or their analyses, must be in a form that is accessible, reliable, and readily usable by future projects. It is likely that the nature of this clearinghouse will be continuously evolving until such time that a common set of reporting guidelines has been fully institutionalized. The reporting guidelines could be for projects, programs, or portfolios. Finally, in order to make the data retrieval user-friendly, the repository of data and best practices (for projects, programs, and portfolios) must be cross-referenced.

Practice. With the availability of the historical data of many years of formalized project management, the EPMO is in an excellent position to develop and disseminate the best practices in project management. Thus, the EPMO will facilitate the efforts to increase knowledge, to improve competencies, and to change attitudes in order to impart a project management mindset to the organization. The guidelines, thus established and disseminated, must contain best practices for managing projects, programs, or portfolios. For mature organizations, these procedures will cover project selection, midstream review, and project cancellation. The EPMO must focus on integrating positive project/program/portfolio practices, promoting the use of recommended tools and templates, and providing guidance and support.

Train. The EPMO would be in charge of development and delivery of training modules on all aspects of project management, hopefully on a proactive and systemic basis. Training modules dealing with enterprise project management issues, such as project selection methods, multi-project resource management, and knowledge management, will be offered only to those team members who are part of the program and portfolio management teams. On the other hand, training modules involving projects will cover all project management knowledge areas dealing with managing individual projects, such as cost, schedule, risk, contracts, communication, teamwork, etc. By supporting the training function, the organization signals to all project personnel that professional development is not only an individual responsibility but is also a corporate responsibility.

2.2 The Path Toward Maturity

In general, the EPMO should facilitate management of projects, individually, in isolation of each other, and in groups of related projects as portfolios or programs. Under ideal circumstances, and in mature organizations, the EPMO does not provide managers and team members for managing projects, programs, or portfolios; rather, the EPMO simply provides guidelines for whomever will carry out those tasks. Given that the EPMO and its concurrent organizational maturity are the foundation of successful portfolio management, if the EPMO is not fully installed, projects of the portfolios will be harder to identify, define, and manage.

If an organization has a fully functional EPMO, more than likely the organization has achieved the mid-levels of project management maturity, partly because of the facilitations that the EPMO would bring to managing projects and partly because of the infrastructure and organizational friendliness that the EPMO would demand for its full-scale operation in team-specific and enterprise-oriented areas. Figure 3 shows the full suite of all of the EPMO functions.

EPMO Functions

- Team-Focused Functions
  - Augment Portfolio/Project Management Team
  - Consult Individual Team Members
  - Mentor Individual Team Members
- Enterprise-Oriented Functions
  - Practice Formalized Portfolio/Project Management
  - Provide a Clearinghouse of Historical Data
  - Train Project Personnel and Functional Management
  - Promote a Project Management Culture

Figure 3

A highly mature organization will have the full complement of the enterprise-oriented functions and few of the team-focused functions (Figure 4), whereas a relatively immature organization will have a forceful suite of the team-focused functions and few of the enterprise-oriented functions (Figure 5). The latter is clearly dependent on team functions and only has rudimentary enterprise functions in place, if any at all. Further, the latter organization uses the enterprise functions sporadically and probably with limited success.

To be realistic, until such time that the organization reaches the apex of maturity, the organization might have both the team-focused and the enterprise-oriented functions, although it is unlikely that an organization's EPMO

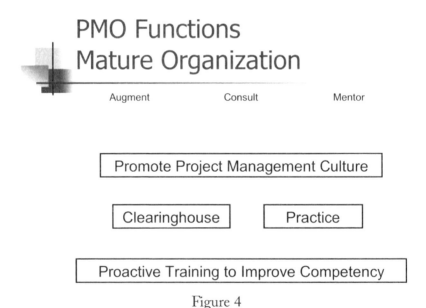

PMO Functions
Mature Organization

Augment   Consult   Mentor

Promote Project Management Culture

Clearinghouse   Practice

Proactive Training to Improve Competency

Figure 4

will have all of these functions with somewhat of an equal weight. One would hope that, in time, the reactive team-focused functions would decrease, while the proactive enterprise-oriented functions would increase. The distinguishing features of a mature organization and an immature organization are the extent to which the organization invokes the team-focused functions by having the EPMO participate directly in project performance and portfolio management, and whether the EPMO's participation includes any of the enterprise-oriented functions.

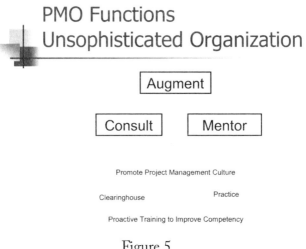

PMO Functions
Unsophisticated Organization

Augment

Consult   Mentor

Promote Project Management Culture

Clearinghouse   Practice

Proactive Training to Improve Competency

Figure 5

If PPM is not sophisticated, chances are that the features of the EPMO are also unsophisticated. In such an unfortunate case, probably projects are selected in an ad-hoc fashion, and they are managed using ad-hoc procedures and rudimentary project management guidelines. It bears repeating that the enterprise-oriented functions of EPMO are prominent in a sophisticated and mature organization, while the team-focused functions of the EPMO are the only visible ones in an immature organization (Figure 6).

Emphasis of PMO Functions

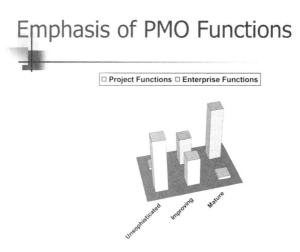

Figure 6

As organizations advance in their project management sophistication, the first attempt at sophistication could be the implementation of some of the features of an EPMO, a metrics system, a program management system, or a portfolio management system. (Figure 7) Given that this incremental approach is somewhat ad-hoc, the naming convention of these functions is not fully consistent across organizations. For example, the portfolio management in one organization could include metrics and program management, while in another organization, it could be simply a semi-formalized organizational process for selecting projects, or yet in a third organization it could be the midstream evaluation and de-activation of individual projects in the portfolio.

Incremental Enhancement Efforts

- Enterprise Project Management Office
- Project Management Office
- Project Office
- Metrics Program
- Portfolio Management
- Program Management

Figure 7

Chapter Summary. It is highly likely that the desire to have a formalized portfolio management function will go hand in hand with the desire to manage the projects within the portfolio as efficiently as possible. These two major function groups will require the assistance, facilitation, and guidance of a full-scale Enterprise Project Management Office.

A typical organization will only need the team-focused function groups of an EPMO, namely augment, mentor, consult. However, organizations that are on a path to maturity might have various forms of the enterprise-oriented function groups, in addition to the team-focused function groups. One would hope that during the journey toward maturity, there would be less emphasis on team-focused function groups and more emphasis on enterprise-oriented function groups. Ultimately, a fully mature organization will only need the enterprise-oriented function groups of the EPMO: promote, archive, practice, and train.

3. Project Portfolio Management Deployment Guidelines

There are two major objectives in implementing a project portfolio management (PPM) system: one—that the implementation should be conducted efficiently and effectively; and two—that the PPM system should meet its own objectives successfully. The motivation for implementing PPM can be from the desire for improvements in operational efficiency, improvements in cost savings, or increased profits. Interestingly enough, an effective PPM system will result in all three, regardless of which motivation was the basis for implementation.

Project portfolio management can be implemented at any level in the organization. Ideally, it is implemented by the Chief Executive Officer (CEO) of the organization and has an impact throughout the entire organization. However, if the organization is not at this stage of its maturity, PPM can be implemented at a distinct organizational level which might be focused at a business sector, government agency, a department, or a division. Alternately, the first attempt at PPM could be by a large program that comprises multiple projects (Figure 1).

PPM Placement

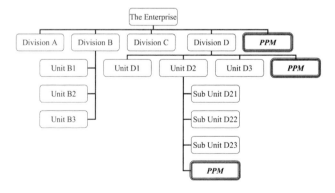

Figure 1

The amount of effort involved in PPM implementation depends on the organization's current maturity level in managing portfolios of projects. If the organization already has a centralized process for management of projects through an Enterprise Project Management Office (EPMO) or the equivalent, the task of implementing a PPM will be smoother and shorter, because, in such a case, PPM implementation would require minor refinements to an existing system. Therefore, as planning is done to implement the PPM, the existence of a distinct method for prioritizing projects should be identified. Thus, depending on the organizational sophistication, the amount of effort necessary to identify and formalize the prioritization process might be a little or a great deal.

If the PPM is established at the highest levels of the organization, the implementation cost can be a major investment. The significance of the magnitude of the investment would be higher if the PPM implementation represents a major cultural change for the organization. However, those organizations in which there is evidence of a high level of maturity in the management of its projects, and that already have an EPMO or Project Management Offices (PMO) in place, may not have to spend any appreciable additional money to establish a formalized PPM process and structure.

Successful implementation will require the efforts of the PPM manager, the staff that will be part of the PPM unit, the people who will participate as members of the Portfolio Review Board (PRB), and the managers that will contribute to the success of the PPM function. Once the PPM process is implemented and operational, it will require periodic outside review to ascertain its effectiveness so that continuous improvements can be made.

The implementation of PPM in the organization should be planned and executed like that of any other project, possibly even more so because its success will impact not only the effectiveness of the organization, but will also prove the value of methodical project management. It should be planned, executed, and monitored with utmost care.

3.1 The Organization's Vision for Project Portfolio Management

Kotter (1995) describes vision as something that helps clarify the direction in which to proceed; it must reflect the organization's cultural values, and it must be meaningful and valid to stakeholders. During the implementation of PPM, everyone must have the same idea as to the importance of projects, and project management, to the organization. Portfolio management sets the stage for a changed approach, one that facilitates the introduction and use of the PPM model and process in the organization. The vision also needs to be revisited periodically to ensure it remains consistent with organizational goals. The vision of each project in the portfolio should be a definitive description independent of the rough planning data that initially describe the project.

The organizational vision for PPM, the objectives to be pursued, the functions to be performed, and the manager for the PPM initiative must be defined as the first step in planning the implementation. An executive at the appropriate level in the organization should issue a short statement describing organizational commitment for PPM based on the organization's vision for PPM to all employees so the initiative is not a surprise. Timely dissemination of the plans for PPM implementation will promote open communications about the PPM, which in turn will facilitate the acceptance of the concept across the organization.

3.2 Goals for Project Portfolio Management

It is necessary to determine the goals for PPM in the organization and the scope of its coverage. During this process, some key questions to consider include:

• Is the purpose of PPM one of a data collection and a reporting mechanism about existing projects at stage gates in the project life cycle through reviews by executive management, or is it to have broader functions affecting strategic planning and decision making for the organization in terms of the various components of the portfolio to pursue, defer, or terminate?
• Is PPM expected to support all of the organization's projects, programs, and other activities, or does it just support a single program or department/division's projects, programs, and other activities?

If the PPM function is to be responsible for all of the enterprise's initiatives, and if its staff is to be empowered to make recommendations for decisions and monitor and control the implementation, it will be institutionalizing best practices throughout the organization. Its broad scope will necessitate a full-time executive-level position reporting to the Chief Projects Officer or even directly to the CEO. However, if the scope is to be limited to a division or department, the functions can be performed by a staff assistant reporting to the head of the EPMO or PMO or to the head of the division or department. Regardless, an integrated project team (IPT), with a project manager, should be established to lead the PPM implementation initiative, along with a core team of approximately three to five people that represent key areas of the business.

For best results, the project manager and IPT members need to be known to the rest of the organization as senior and experienced contributors. Time must be set aside for them to develop the implementation plans for PPM. Approximately three to six weeks of dedicated effort is recommended, as this implementation cannot be part of an individual's existing responsibilities. The project manager should hold a formal kickoff meeting of the IPT. The individual selected as the project manager, as well as the IPT members, will need excellent communications skills to converse with executives about the importance of portfolio management to the organization.

Like most of the current portfolio management processes and models, PPM includes direct and regular intervention by upper management, because although the areas of analysis and evaluation are highlighted, the details of such analysis are not sufficient for delegating the task to a portfolio team (Figure 2).

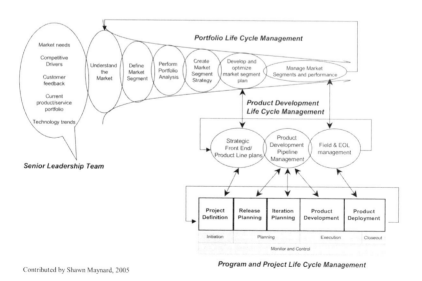

Contributed by Shawn Maynard, 2005

Figure 2

As noted earlier, one of the better known portfolio management models is the stage-gate model proposed by Cooper, Edgett, and Kleinschmidt (2001). Probably the most valuable facet of this approach is the identification of the milestones at which the validity of the project needs to be affirmed for it to go forward. Naturally, the number and texture of project phases would be different in different industries, maybe even in different projects. Accordingly, the nature of the inter-phase tests, which will be conducted at the gates, would be industry-specific and even project-specific.

The prioritization of authorized projects will have to be revisited on a regular basis. Most of the current portfolio management models are heavily dependent on the project schedule and for the judgment that would need to be exercised at those different points in the life of the project. Depending on the nature of the enterprise, and the nature of the project, the occasions and frequency by which the portfolio and/or a single project will be examined can be predicted by the business imperatives of the portfolio, or by the target milestones of a single project.

Early project selection methods were not sophisticated in the sense that they used quantitative techniques such as linear programming, non-linear programming, or integer programming, and decision trees (Cooper, Edgett, and Kleinschmidt, 2001). They were also unsophisticated in the sense that they did not consider many variables in the same model. Notwithstanding, given that these techniques did not deliver a definite solution to the problem of prioritizing projects on a massive scale, many mapping techniques have been used to help the portfolio management personnel visualize and compare different aspects of the projects in the portfolio, using bubbles, circles, and a variety of labels for the projects groups (Figure 3).

Examples of such depictions are the risk-reward diagrams that use four quadrants for the four combinations of high-low risk and reward. In risk-reward diagrams, the cost of a project depicted by the size of the circle (Kendall, Wysocki, Frame). Additionally, the pattern in the circles could represent one or two attributes of the project, and different icons can be used to depict strategic fit of the project. The circles can be replaced by ellipses if the exact values are not known and only a range estimate is available for one of the two variables. Another interesting plot is one where business strength and market opportunity are plotted against each other, with projects plotted with their cost or other attributes shown by icons or patterns.

Displaying
Portfolio Project Attributes

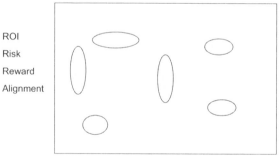

ROI
Risk
Reward
Alignment

Cost, Reward, Risk, Payback Period

Figure 3

3.2.1 Organizational Maturity in
Project Portfolio Management

The IPT, the EPMO staff, or an independent third party, should conduct a review of the current status of the organization's maturity and organizational attitude toward portfolio management to provide a baseline from which to measure future improvements. This maturity assessment is not one that focuses on the maturity of its project management processes, such as that outlined in Project Management Institute's Organization Project Management Maturity Model (PMI, 2003), nor is it an assessment of project management maturity following the tenets in the Software Engineering Institutes' Capability Maturity Model Integration (CMMI). Rather, its focus is to assess existing approaches that may or may not be in place in terms of identifying portfolio components to pursue, methods to use to decide which components to pursue, monitoring and controlling activities once components of the portfolio are under way, and methods to determine whether existing portfolio components should be terminated early. The assessment examines the effectiveness of any processes and procedures that may be in place for portfolio management, and whether or not these processes and procedures are followed. It provides the foundation and guidance for further advancement in portfolio management. Figure 4 presents organizations that are at different levels of maturity as it relates to the handling of their portfolios.

Following principles of a staged maturity model, Appendix A contains an instrument that can be used as a first approximation of the level of maturity in order to identify key practices that require management's attention. Using this approach, higher maturity levels will signify more effective processes and procedures that follow an objective basis to the PPM process. By contrast, lower maturity levels are consistent with an organization that lacks such processes and in which ad hoc methods are used to select portfolio components, allocate resources and funding to them, and evaluate their continued significance. Strengths and weaknesses can be identified through the maturity assessment process.

Maturity Levels

- **Level 1** *If a formalized project portfolio management unit exists in the enterprise, it is very modest and not very sophisticated. It will probably be commissioned to develop basic practices for project selection and project performance.*

- **Level 2** *The PPM unit will develop some standard processes and practices for PPM. This unit will probably handle project prioritization processes as well as cross-project critical processes. Further, the PPM unit will probably attempt to institutionalize the PPM practice across the entire enterprise.*

- **Level 3** *The PPM unit will establish and monitor use of a complete project portfolio management methodology. Extensive training will be provided to all personnel who would be involved in this process.*

- **Level 4** *The PPM unit will promote the use of a comprehensive, and possibly singular, portfolio management system across the enterprise. PPM will be fully integrated into business processes as part of the adoption of the management-by-projects concept.*

- **Level 5** *The PPM unit will monitor the enterprises' portfolio, which will probably be running at peak efficiency, for opportunities to recommend continuous improvements in models, indices, processes, and procedures.*

Figure 4

3.2.2 Baseline Data on Portfolio Components

It is important to ascertain whether the existing programs and projects are supportive of current strategic goals and objectives. Further, to obtain information on organizational resource use, resource allocation data need to be collected on ongoing operational activities. Along with the results of the maturity assessment of portfolio management, this inventory information should be compiled into a report and/or presentation to the executive sponsors. Appendix B, Portfolio Management Assessment Report, contains an outline for a report, or a presentation, dealing with such a review.

In addition to the maturity assessment, baseline data on portfolio components must be collected, especially since many organizations do not have an accurate picture of:

- The number of programs and projects that are under way at any given time
- The people who are supporting each project
- How the projects were selected
- How long each project has been under way
- Scheduled completion date, total cost, and complexity of each project
- Interdependencies among programs and projects and their sponsors

3.2.3 Portfolio Manager Charter

A charter for Portfolio Manager should be prepared and issued. The charter should describe the goals and objectives for portfolio management in the organization, the Portfolio Manager's level of authority and responsibility, key milestones, major risks, constraints, and assumptions regarding the portfolio management function in the organization. The charter then sets the stage for the remainder of the PPM activities. Ideally, it should be prepared and issued by the Chairperson of the organization's PRB. The PRB Chairperson should obtain signoffs from the other members of the PRB as well as any other key executives in the rest of the organization. See Appendix C for a sample template for the Portfolio Manager's Charter.

Following the issuance of the charter, the roles and responsibilities of the PRB also should be described, and members of the PRB should be identified. If, as recommended, the PPM function is an enterprise-wide function, the Chairperson of the PRB should be at the highest level of the organization, with other members representing key business functional units. The Portfolio Manager should serve as the Secretary of the PRB. A charter for the PRB also should be prepared and issued. See Appendix D—Portfolio Review Board Charter for a sample template for this charter.

3.2.4 Roles and Responsibilities

There are two sets of duties that must be identified during the planning stages of PPM: implementation and operational. Implementation duties outline the duties related to the implementation tasks. Operational duties describe the functions that will be performed by those personnel who will manage the portfolio(s) of the organization, and who will make continuous improvements to the sophistication of this system.

The operational roles and responsibilities must be well defined with the agreement and participation of the stakeholders of the PPM system. The Portfolio Manager, portfolio management team, and the members of the PRB should be cognizant of the scope of their responsibilities and their desired interaction with others in the organization. As Kendall and Rollins (2003) note, since people use processes to complete work, if the portfolio management process is successful, people must recognize and commit to their specific roles and responsibilities. These roles and responsibilities must be well defined.

A brief list of the functions to be performed in portfolio management by the EPMO staff is to:

• Validate the organization's strategic direction
• Participate in the continuous improvement of the project prioritization models
• Conduct regular examinations of the organization's competitive position
• Provide best practices for monitoring project performance

A brief list of the duties of the Portfolio Manager is to:

• Conduct project prioritization on a regular basis
• Monitor portfolio performance
• Manage the portfolio mix
• Maintain a balance in the portfolio of projects in light of business goals
• Allocate resources in light of business goals
• Conduct consistent reviews of portfolio progress
• Draft portfolio reports
• Distribute reports in accordance with the communications plan

A brief list of the duties of Project Managers of the projects in the portfolio is to:

• Develop the project charter for the initial prioritization process
• Develop the project business case with input from the EPMO, upper management, and the portfolio manager
• Manage the ongoing project performance
• Enhance the values of the project indices for the regular re-prioritization efforts

Appendix E presents a detailed set of the duties of the Portfolio Manager according to the Aligning and Monitoring and Controlling Process Groups following the format in the Project Management Institute's *Portfolio Management Standard* (PMI, 2006). The duties are described in three levels that correspond to the sophistication of the organization. As such, the duties at each level build on those of the previous level. Competencies for the Portfolio Manager are detailed in Appendix F. Roles and responsibilities of the PRB, and other Portfolio stakeholders, are contained in Appendix G.

3.3 Project Portfolio Management Scope Statement

Once the PPM IPT's work is complete, the Portfolio Manager position should be filled. The work done to date by the PPM IPT should be turned over to this manager. The PRB should be established at this point.

The Portfolio Manager should then prepare a scope statement to describe the organization's intent and the purpose of PPM. The scope statement expands the elements of the charters of the Portfolio Manager and the PRB. Thus, the scope statement would describe success criteria for the organizational PPM. The scope statement would also include the specifications of the PPM functions that will be provided, and the resources that will be allocated to support portfolio management. Other data that might be included in the scope statement are implementation details such as the cost, initial defined risks, schedule milestones, and necessary approvals. This PPM scope statement, similar to that of a project scope statement, must be progressively elaborated as the PPM function evolves in the organization.

3.4 Project Portfolio Management Work Breakdown Structure

Once the scope statement is complete and approved, the Portfolio Manager should prepare a Work Breakdown Structure (WBS) to show the various deliverables of the PPM project. This WBS will serve as a framework for PPM activities throughout the organization. Appendix H contains a sample WBS template following the PMI Portfolio Management Standard (PMI, 2006).

3.5 Portfolio Management Plan

After the charter, scope statement, and WBS are developed, the Portfolio Manager should prepare a portfolio management plan to guide the operations of the portfolio management staff and the PRB. The plan should describe the objectives for portfolio management with specific milestones and completion targets as to when each function will be fully operational. The implementation portion of the portfolio management plan should include a schedule network diagram, bar chart, and a cost estimate. Additionally, the operational plan should include details of roles and responsibilities and specifics of interfaces with project managers, program managers, functional managers, the EPMO staff, and the PRB. Appendix I includes a checklist that could be used during the planning and implementation of the PPM system.

Since not everything can be done at once, the plan should be prepared to show near-term, intermediate, and long-term milestones. Figure 5 includes typical milestones that would need to be planned for the implementation phase of the PPM.

The Portfolio Manager should prepare a communications management plan that details the key stakeholders, their information requirements, and when information on portfolio management will be provided, during the implementation of the system and during the operation of the system. See Appendix J for a sample communications plan template. In accordance with the distribution structure of the communications management plan, the portfolio management plan should be distributed to stakeholders for information, review, comment, and approval.

Orientation sessions and meetings should be arranged with the various stakeholders to explain the mission of the portfolio management staff and the objectives for the organizational portfolio management system. Similar to the staff of an EPMO, the portfolio management staff should be viewed as a complementary and supportive unit in the organization.

PPM Implementation Milestones

- First noticeable improvement
- Intermediate benefits
  - Short term, three months
    - Overall organizational impact
    - Immediate methodology needs
  - Mid term, three to six months
    - Roll out operational PPM
    - Support function
  - Long term, beyond six months
    - Fully functional PPM
    - Implement project portfolio database
    - Formalize report generation and distribution

Figure 5

As one of its earliest activities, the portfolio management staff must establish the PPM model that the organization will follow during the prioritization reviews. Additionally, the staff will need to link the portfolio management processes to the organization's annual budgeting process. Finally, it would be prudent to use this model within a department or division, to assess its effectiveness, before implementing it throughout the organization.

3.6 Portfolio Management Information System

The Portfolio Manager must design, develop, implement, and maintain a portfolio management information system. Kendall and Rollins (2003) suggest that this system contain documented details of both tactical and strategic data. Tactical processes address ongoing projects, while strategic processes focus on selection of new projects or termination of existing projects in light of organizational objectives. They recommend that the system consist of policies, processes, techniques, tools, plans, and controls for portfolio management.

The information system serves as a repository of information on all of the projects in the portfolio. Data contained in the system would need to be reliable and accurate. Therefore, a process is required to ensure that data are submitted when due, and that data are updated as required. Data entry should use consistent templates and be straightforward. The system should have the ability to sort and filter data for use in preparing status reports for the various portfolio management stakeholders.

Data should be entered only once even if used in different parts of the system. Further, the data should be aggregated to meet the requirements of different stakeholders in the PPM process. The system should also be designed such that it can conveniently track data trends concerning the status of projects within the portfolio. These trend data will be an excellent addendum to the documented accounts of the corrective or preventive actions that are taken for the projects of the portfolio.

A significant requirement of this system is the definition of the interfaces to other systems of the organization such as project management, business development or opportunity management (including both sales and marketing), accounting, financial management, and human resource management. If the ease of integration between common data items within these systems is insufficient, the portfolio management information system can potentially serve as the catalyst for the enhancement of the data integration process.

At a minimum, the system should collect and report the following data elements for each component in the portfolio:

• Identification number
• Component name
• Date component was approved to be part of the organization's portfolio
• Category within the portfolio
• Component description
    • Objectives
    • Link to the organization's strategic objectives
    • Manager
    • Sponsor
    • Milestones
    • Original schedule end date
    • Current schedule end date
    • Key milestones
    • Dates for stage-gate reviews
    • Stage-gate review decisions
    • Cost
    • Original budget/investment
    • Current budget
• Resource requirements
    • Original resource requirements

• Current resource requirements
• Original rank within the portfolio
• Current rank within the portfolio

3.7 Portfolio Review Board Meetings

Working with the PRB, the Portfolio Manager should develop a revolving schedule and a generic agenda for the PRB meetings. One of the subtle advantages of holding regular PPM meetings is that the PPM process will come to be viewed as a permanent fixture and as a strategic necessity in the organization. Additionally, if meetings are held on a regular basis, the Board members can ensure that the portfolio priorities are regularly realigned with the changes to the strategic goals and objectives.

The Portfolio Manager is responsible for documenting the decisions of the Board and for distributing and communicating decisions of the Review Board throughout the organization. This documentation will show new projects to be pursued, projects to be deferred, projects to be cancelled, and projects to be continued but at a different priority within the portfolio.

The Portfolio Manager also is responsible for tracking open issues and action items that arise during Board meetings. This is especially necessary if a decision is made to continue a project, but the project is one that requires corrective or preventive action in order to meet its projected return and contribution. The Portfolio Manager then must monitor the actions that are taken and contact the Board members if it appears that the root cause of the problem is too great, and that the project may need to be cancelled.

During each meeting, the status of projects currently in the portfolio should be reviewed, as well as the description of new projects or other components that are potentially to be added to the portfolio. The business case must be made for each proposed portfolio component in order to facilitate the determination of whether or not it should be pursued. Appendix K contains a template for submitting a proposed component to the PPM system.

The Board will review specific portfolio components, which are already in progress, to determine if they should continue to receive resources. The progress of the component will be reviewed in the light of the business case of that particular component.

Board members will assess whether each project improves the financial position of the overall portfolio in some way. If the results are satisfactory, then the project moves into the next stage of its life cycle, and the additional investment will be authorized. The Portfolio Manager should prepare guidelines for use by project and program managers during the gate review process. These questions are designed to ascertain the progress of the project, and to determine whether continued support is warranted.

Over time, the PPM process will require outside review to ascertain its effectiveness so that continuous improvements can be made to the PPM structure and its processes. See Appendix L for suggested items to review.

Chapter Summary. Implementation of a portfolio management system must be conducted just like any other project, but even more so because this implementation will prove the advantages of proper planning and proper execution for a capability improvement project. A successful portfolio management process will depend on fully delineated roles and responsibilities that are consistent with the organizational support for this initiative.

The implementation of a portfolio management system will primarily formalize the manner by which projects are prioritized, funded, and managed. Hopefully, given time, a PPM system will result in improvements in the way in which new projects are identified, and the approach by which the organization supports the activities of the project team in crafting the deliverable as close to the strategic vision as possible.

Appendix A

Maturity in Project Portfolio Management

This instrument provides a preliminary determination of the maturity of project portfolio management (PPM) in an organization. If the attributes of the organization are such that the responses to more than 75% of the statements in each level are affirmative, then it is highly likely that the organizational maturity is at that level.

The Organization is at Level 1
If Most of These Statements Describe Your Portfolio Management Environment

• Projects are not selected according to set criteria.
• The organization lacks a strategic plan.
• Projects are not linked to organizational goals.
• People can propose and execute projects as desired.
• Minor projects can escalate into major undertakings.
• Many projects are not officially closed.
• Many projects continue indefinitely and take on a life of their own.
• New requirements lead to new projects that are not officially authorized.
• Effort can be duplicated as similar projects can be under way elsewhere in the organization.
• Some people feel they are locked into the same project for years at a time without an end, and at times without recognition of the importance of the project, leading to poor morale.
• The organization does not have an inventory of all of its current projects.
• Basic information is not available concerning the organization's projects.
• Project reviews are not held.
• A Project Management Office (PMO) has not been established.
• There is an unrealistic assessment of the capability to complete projects and to continue ongoing operations.
• Resource overloading is the norm, as the organization lacks a resource management information system.

• Project and program reporting requirements are inconsistent.
• Reporting requirements are mandated; however, there is limited understanding as to how data collected actually are used.
• There are few, if any, processes or procedures available concerning portfolio management.
• Few, if any, people have had training in the concepts of portfolio management.

The Organization is at Level 2
If Most of These Statements Describe Your Project Portfolio Management Environment

• The organization's management reviews and approves new projects to become part of its portfolio.
• Interdependencies among projects are not known.
• Resource over-commitments are not known.
• The focus is on the project, rather than on what is needed to achieve it successfully.
• The budgeting process is managed separately for each project.
• The organization lacks a mission statement or vision statement, and at times the link between the project and the organization's strategic plan is not known.
• Most of the projects that are selected are ones with a short-term (less than six month) payoff.
• The project review process is cursory and focuses primarily on completed and upcoming milestones.
• Project reporting is standardized.
• A project management information system is under development.
• Resources are negotiated on a project-by-project basis.
• A limited number of people in the organization have taken training in portfolio management.
• A PMO has been established at the division or equivalent level.
• There is some effort under way to establish a portfolio management process at a local level, but there is not a standard PPM approach in place in the organization.

The Organization is at Level 3
If Most of These Statements Describe Your Project Portfolio Management Environment

• There is a sponsor or champion for portfolio management in the enterprise.
• Portfolio management follows a defined process for decision making.
• Criteria have been established for use in making selection decisions among components in the portfolio (projects, programs, and ongoing operations).
• A list of the components in the portfolio is available and maintained.
• Analysis of the pursuit of different types of components in the portfolio is conducted.
• Each portfolio component is categorized with common criteria.
• Each portfolio component is focused on determining the needs of the business.
• A process has been established that enables costs, risks, and benefits of possible components to be evaluated.
• A system has been set up to schedule and balance resource requirements.
• A system is in place so that individual components in the portfolio can be either expanded or contracted.
• A system is in place so that resources can be reallocated to support the more important components.
• A process is in place to submit a proposal for consideration to the portfolio.
• There is an approach to rank or prioritize components in the portfolio.
• There is a standard approach to report component progress.
• There is a standard approach to prepare a business case for each proposed component and for continuing with ongoing operations in house, rather than using outsourcing.
• Common metrics are collected so that progress, performance, and dependencies are regularly monitored and tracked.
• Standard criteria are used to assess whether a proposed component should not be pursued.
• Executives view projects as groups of related initiatives, rather than as a series of isolated islands.
• Dependencies among components are identified and managed.

• An ongoing review is conducted of projects in the portfolio, with components being de-selected or terminated as appropriate.
• Non value-added components can be identified.
• Duplicate projects are identified; resources are concentrated on a few high-value projects, rather than on projects that may no longer be required or that should have been terminated.
• Each person understands the priority of the portfolio component he or she is assigned to work on in the organization.
• Project and program managers recognize how their work is measured and valued, as do functional managers; both can accept and receive changes based on changing business conditions.
• Portfolio components are scheduled and funded accordingly, and prioritization decisions communicated throughout the organization.
• At risk and/or under-performing portfolio components can be easily evaluated.
• Key metrics for monitoring and controlling components have been agreed upon and are used.
• The portfolio shares and allocates resources among components.
• A communications management plan has been prepared and is followed for PPM.

The Organization is at Level 4
If Most of These Statements Describe Your Project Portfolio Management Environment

• The organization's executives recognize the value of PPM.
• The organization's executives recognize the value of each component in the portfolio.
• Categories of portfolio components are established.
• Portfolio components are aligned with strategic objectives.
• The portfolio management information system is set up to contain information on the business initiatives.
• Metrics are available to measure the ongoing value of portfolio components.
• Systems are available to support PPM with accurate and timely data to show performance across projects as well as infrastructure investments; a digital dashboard is set up and maintained regularly.

• Trend analyses of the value of portfolio components are conducted.
• Analyses are conducted regularly to determine the complexity of the portfolio, to address unique challenges, and to ensure that there is a balance among projects in the categories established for alignment.
• Prioritization is done in order that only the most valuable work is authorized.
• Projects in progress are scrutinized according to similar criteria/rigor.
• Progress on portfolio components is tracked across the entire organization.
• Critical activities to be monitored are known with standard definitions.
• A rigorous risk assessment is performed of each component in the portfolio.
• The portfolio is continually reviewed and changed as needed to produce the highest returns; focus has shifted from the cost of the project to one that examines its significance strategically to the organization and its value.
• The impact of resources and skills limitations and their effect on the portfolio is known.
• All work is scrutinized so that people cannot, on their own, implement their own pet projects and personally approve them.
• People have an organizational focus, rather than a departmental or sector focus, so that projects can be prioritized for the enterprise.
• People throughout the organization understand the portfolio management process that is followed and why it is being used.
• Decisions are communicated throughout the organization, with open communication the norm.
• People in the organization recognize that change is inevitable and can easily embrace it.
• Interdependencies of benefits among the various portfolio components are recognized and known.
• A portfolio governance process is in place through a Portfolio Review Board or similar group.
• Actions proposed are routinely implemented and followed up on to assess impact.
• PPM is a separate process from the annual planning and budgeting process so that it is done on a continual basis, rather than on an annual basis.
• Initiatives are interdependent even though there are different payoffs, risks, and opportunities.

• Trends and problem areas can be easily addressed so there is insight into the existing portfolio.
• There is a balance among the various categories in the portfolio, and the balancing process is known throughout the organization.
• The PPM process enables the identification of problem areas quickly to focus management attention and potential resource allocation decisions.
• Established decision-making processes to select components are followed.
• The portfolio information system provides an easy-to-use, interactive filtering system.
• A Portfolio Manager reports to the Chief Projects Officer or equivalent of the organization.
• Key stakeholders receive regular assessments of the health of the portfolio.

The Organization is at Level 5
If Most of These Statements Describe Your Project Portfolio Management Environment

• The Portfolio Manager actively manages the portfolio to meet changing business needs.
• The Portfolio Manager has prepared and issued a process improvement plan for PPM.
• PPM is recognized as the key to provide a faster and more effective response to changing conditions.
• PPM optimizes investment decisions by prioritizing and balancing the work to be done within the portfolio.
• Investments, organizational capability, and capacity are optimized with projects and programs.
• Resources are prioritized and allocated for maximum benefit.
• The portfolio encompasses all the work under way in the organization.
• Continual re-planning is the norm.
• The portfolio management process itself is routinely analyzed for continuous improvement.
• Portfolio management decisions are made within the context of enterprise strategy and goals.
• Prioritization is done across the entire enterprise; all subordinate organizations collaborate on an ongoing basis.

- The organization's culture is both collaborative and communicative.
- People are encouraged at all levels to submit ideas and suggestions to foster continuous improvement to the PPM process.
- The value of project outcomes and alignment with business strategy is actively managed.
- PPM ensures that each project's contribution to the organization is known, including how to recognize whether the project is a success.
- The PPM process can be easily adapted to changing circumstances.
- Environmental constraints that may affect the portfolio are known.
- Continuous improvement to the PPM process is the norm.
- Portfolio metrics are related to other metrics in the organization.
- The PPM process is integrated with the strategic planning process.
- The portfolio information system interfaces with other systems in the organization.
- Key performance indicators are refined as required.
- Criteria are used to evaluate the effectiveness of PPM.
- The Portfolio Manager is a member of the organization's executive management team.
- The portfolio management system is continually reviewed to ensure that it is aligned with corporate strategy.
- Realignment of existing portfolio components is expected and is an ongoing process.

Appendix B

Project Portfolio Management Assessment Report Template

1. Scope of Assessment Activities
Inventory current programs and projects
Selection process, resource allocation, interdependencies, complexity, status
Inventory resources allocated to ongoing activities
Determine project portfolio management maturity
According to maturity levels
According to:
    Aligning Process Group
        Identification
        Categorization
        Evaluation
        Selection
        Prioritization
        Portfolio Balancing
        Authorization
    Monitoring and Controlling Process Group
        Periodic Review and Reporting
        Strategic Change
Interview selected staff
Review documentation
Prepare and deliver a findings and recommendations report

2. Interviews Held
Interviewees
Name and title

3. Documentation Reviewed
Policies, procedures, guidelines
Specific program and project data

4. Assessment Team
List Name, phone, e-mail

5. Program / Project Inventory
Number of programs by business unit/department
Number of projects in each program
    On Schedule
    Within Budget
    Within Scope
Strategic goals supported
Average resources per project
Average number of interdependencies per project

6. Resource Inventory
Number of resources per business unit / department
    Allocated to programs
    Allocated to projects
    Allocated to ongoing activities
    By areas of expertise
    By years of experience

7. Key Portfolio Management Strengths
List the key strengths in portfolio management as noted in the maturity assessment
    Aligning Process Group
    Monitoring and Controlling Process Group

8. Key Portfolio Management Weaknesses
List key weaknesses in portfolio management
    Aligning Process Group
    Monitoring and Controlling Process Group

9. Primary Recommendations
Identification
    Strengths
    Weaknesses
Categorization
    Strengths
    Weaknesses

Evaluation
  Strengths
  Weaknesses
Selection
  Strengths
  Weaknesses
Prioritization
  Strengths
  Weaknesses
Portfolio Balancing
  Strengths
  Weaknesses
Authorization
  Strengths
  Weaknesses
Periodic Review and Reporting
  Strengths
  Weaknesses
Strategic Change
  Strengths
  Weaknesses

Appendix C

Portfolio Manager

Sample Charter Template

Portfolio Manager	Name	Phone	E-Mail
Goals: State the goals for portfolio management in the organization.			
Objectives: State the objectives for the current year for portfolio management.			
Authority and Responsibility: State the Portfolio Manager's authority. Describe the Portfolio Manager's responsibilities.			
Portfolio Management Team: Identify the Portfolio Management Team members, including the members of the Portfolio Review Board with contact information.			
General Approach: Describe the general approach for portfolio management in the organization.			
Constraints: State any applicable constraints.			
Assumptions: State any applicable assumptions.			
Tentative Portfolio Risk Management Plan: Describe the general approach to risk management in the organization. Describe the risk management tools to be used. Identify the key risks and response plans as well as owners for each risk.			

Portfolio Manager	Name	Phone	E-Mail
Tentative Portfolio Schedule Management Plan: Describe the milestones for the coming year. List schedule interfaces. Describe schedule reviews, status reports, and analysis methods. Describe how the schedule will be maintained. Describe how schedule changes will be controlled.			
Tentative Portfolio Cost Management Plan: State the portfolio resources and costs. Describe cost reviews, status reports, and analysis methods. Describe how cost changes will be controlled.			
Tentative Portfolio Quality Management Plan: Describe the overall approach to quality. State measurement criteria, objectives, and thresholds. Describe quality assurance and quality control techniques and tools to be used. List key metrics to be reported.			
Tentative Portfolio Management Training Plan: Describe the necessary training to introduce portfolio management to the organization. Describe the training schedule			
Tentative Portfolio Management Evaluation Methods: Describe how the portfolio management process will be evaluated and how progress toward objectives and goals will be measured.			
Approvals – Name Date: Portfolio Review Board Chairperson Portfolio Review Board Member 1 Portfolio Review Board Member 2 Portfolio Review Board Member N Portfolio Manager			

Appendix D

Portfolio Review Board

Charter Template

Portfolio Review Board (PRB) Chairperson	Phone	Cell	E-mail
PRB Member #1	Phone	Cell	E-mail
PRB Member #2	Phone	Cell	E-mail
PRB Member #3	Phone	Cell	E-mail
Portfolio Manager Manager	Phone	Cell	E-mail
Project Portfolio Management (PPM) Goals and Objectives			
Overview of the PRB's Roles and Responsibilities			
Description of the Portfolio Manager's Interfaces with the PRB			
Frequency of PRB Meetings			
Assumptions			
Constraints			
Major Risks			
Communication Process			
Approvals:			
PRB	Signature		Date
PRB Member #1	Signature		Date
PRB Member #2	Signature		Date
PRB Member #N	Signature		Date

Appendix E

Duties of the Portfolio Manager

Task	Duties in a Typical Organization	Duties in a Maturing Organization	Duties in a Mature Organization
Identify	Maintains a list of ongoing components within the portfolio Maintains a list of proposed components to the portfolio since the last Portfolio Review Board (PRB) meeting Based on the number of proposed components, suggests that the PRB be convened if a scheduled meeting is not upcoming Provides input to the development of the organization's strategic plan and vision Prepares a structured method to classify components of the portfolio Notes the category or class of each proposed component to the portfolio Prepares and maintains descriptions of each portfolio component Prepares templates for component descriptions Prepares a template for use in submitting proposed components to the portfolio Maintains a list of rejected or deferred components in the portfolio for possible resubmission at a later time	Develops the project portfolio management process (PPM) including the rules and procedures for the PRB Participates in the development of the organization's strategic plan and vision Prepares a stakeholder management plan relative to portfolio management Establishes a process to determine available resource capacity (financial, human, and asset) in the organization Compares ongoing components in the portfolio with proposed additions to it	Leads the development of the organization's strategic plan and vision Coordinates the PPM process with other processes in the organization Establishes and maintains relationships with key stakeholders as the PPM process is introduced Determines resource capacity in the organization Rejects proposed portfolio components that do not fit within the process that has been established

Task	Duties in a Typical Organization	Duties in a Maturing Organization	Duties in a Mature Organization
Catego-rize	Suggests criteria for portfolio component decisions Ensures each component is placed in only one category in the portfolio Generates tables, charts, and graphs based on portfolio components for use by the PRB and other key stakeholders	Develops qualitative and quantitative criteria for the portfolio model Determines the categorization criteria Ensures that components in a given category in the portfolio can be measured in common ways	Establishes criteria for PRB decisions Determines strategic categories that each component in the portfolio will support Determines the importance of customer satisfaction as part of the establishment of the mix of components in the portfolio Compares components to the categorization criteria If a proposed component cannot be categorized, determines whether it is of such importance that the categorization system requires revision so that this component can be retained on the list Establishes metrics or key performance indicators for portfolio management
Evaluate	Establishes quantitative indices for PPM Determines resource availability Gathers information for use in evaluating components for use in the selection process Summarizes information for each component Prepares graphs, documents, charts, and recommendations for the PRB and other key stakeholders to support the decision-making process based on the portfolio model	Establishes qualitative indices for PPM Determines the desired level of accuracy for the data collection process Makes recommendations for the selection process Calculates a total score for each proposed component according to the portfolio model	Establishes evaluation methodologies for proposed components Establishes the portfolio model with weighted key criteria Evaluates each proposed component according to the portfolio model Prepares a list of evaluated and approved components for each category in the portfolio

Task	Duties in a Typical Organization	Duties in a Maturing Organization	Duties in a Mature Organization
Select	Establishes a process to ensure updates are received concerning changes in the organization's strategic plan, such as whether or not a goal is no longer valid, or if a new goal is to be added Maintains the list of categorized and evaluated proposed components	Prepares a list of components to be pursued in the portfolio, to be postponed, or to be cancelled based on the evaluation process Makes recommendations for the prioritization process	Negotiates agreements with stakeholders concerning the portfolio components to be pursued Defines the human resource, financial, and asset capacity of the organization to support new components proposed for the portfolio
Prioritize	Confirms that the component classification follows the established criteria Maintains the prioritized list of the components Prepares "what if"/scenario analyses of different strategies during the prioritization process	Establishes key performance indicators to determine the viability of the components in the portfolio Ranks proposed components within each category Assigns scores and weighting criteria Makes recommendations on the components to receive the highest priority	Establishes constraints and assumptions for the PPM process Establishes proposed component ranking criteria Determines the components to receive the highest priority in the portfolio
Balance	Reviews the portfolio system for balance among components Performs "what if"/scenario analyses concerning various scenarios in the portfolio to determine the ultimate value proposition for the organization Determines similarities and synergies between existing components in the portfolio Maintains the master list of approved, deferred, or terminated portfolio components	Relates the organization's strategic plan and vision to the components of the portfolio Performs risk analyses concerning components of the portfolio Makes recommendations to the PRB concerning the portfolio component mix with the greatest potential Makes recommendations to the PRB to maintain the portfolio as is or to adjust it	Aligns the portfolio management system with corporate strategy Ensures each component in the portfolio is one that will achieve the organization's strategic goals Ensures stakeholder interests are balanced and managed Determines the organization's risk profile Determines the portfolio component mix with the greatest potential Determines whether existing portfolio components require realignment

Task	Duties in a Typical Organization	Duties in a Maturing Organization	Duties in a Mature Organization
Authorize	Provides budget requirement information for each component Provides resource requirement information for each component Maintains the active component inventory Circulates changes to the components concerning resource allocations according to the communications management plan	Issues the list of portfolio components in priority order Communicates portfolio decisions to stakeholders Communicates expected results for each selected component Documents decisions to remove or not include components in the portfolio Prepares and maintains a list of the key deliverables and expected outcomes of the portfolio	Makes decisions concerning components to pursue or continue based on optimization strategies Makes decisions concerning components in the portfolio that should be terminated Makes decisions concerning resource allocation for components in the portfolio Reallocates budgets and resources for terminated components Determines whether performance changes are warranted for components in the portfolio and communicates any updated performance expectations to the stakeholders
Reporting and Review	Establishes a project portfolio information system Prepares, issues, and maintains a portfolio management communications plan Gathers and updates key portfolio performance indicators Provides stakeholders with regular reports on assessments of the portfolio's health and each component's contribution to it Reports progress toward established goals Feeds back information to the strategic planning process	Regularly measures the value of each component in the portfolio to the organization's strategic goals and key performance indicators Establishes a portfolio management reporting system Provides metrics to appropriate stakeholders Establishes a regular cycle for portfolio reviews Provides direction to component owners based on the decisions of the PRB Makes recommendations concerning portfolio rebalancing of components for upcoming reviews	Revises management approaches based on outcomes of the PPM process Establishes portfolio management metrics Relates portfolio metrics to other metrics collected in the organization Integrates the portfolio reporting system with other reporting systems in the organization Ensures alignment of the portfolio with business strategy and resource use Establishes governance standards for the PRB

Task	Duties in a Typical Organization	Duties in a Maturing Organization	Duties in a Mature Organization
	Recognizes the value of high-level project reporting Maintains information on available resources and portfolio priorities Identifies environmental constraints that may affect the portfolio Prepares and issues minutes and action items from meetings of the PRB Documents decisions of the PRB Prepares reports on component progress and forecasts of work in the next reporting period Prepares trend analyses of resource use	Recommends appropriate changes to the component selection criteria Recommends changes to the portfolio review process Recommends appropriate changes to the selection criteria Updates key performance indicators	Recommends appropriate changes to the organization's strategic plan Makes changes to the component selection criteria Makes changes to the portfolio review process Refines selection criteria as appropriate to ensure effective resource allocation Refines key performance indicators as required
Strategic Change	Evaluates qualitative and quantitative benefits of the portfolio Maintains information concerning changes to the organization's strategic goals or plan Recognizing that PPM is a culture change to the organization, conducts orientation sessions with key stakeholders concerning PPM and specific roles and responsibilities	Determines whether or not portfolio management approaches are successful Facilitates meetings of the PRB Monitors benefit realization Maintains visibility of the key stakeholders into the PPM process	Drives the definition of the organization's strategic goals based on the portfolio management process Establishes criteria to evaluate PPM success

Appendix F

Competencies of the Portfolio Manager

Task	Competencies for a Typical Organization	Competencies for a Maturing Organization	Competencies for a Mature Organization
Identify	Strategic planning	Strategic management	Transformational management
Categorize	Analytical skills	Consensus management	Strategic alignment
Evaluate	Analytical skills Evaluation methodologies Sensitivity analysis "What if" analysis Risk analysis	Resource management Risk management Constraint analysis Assumptions analysis	Sophisticated analytical tools
Select	Communications skills	Communications management	Negotiation skills Stakeholder management
Prioritize	Benefit measurement methods Analytical skills	Resource management	Stakeholder management
Balance	Communications skills Sensitivity analysis "What if" analysis Risk analysis	Benefit management Risk management	Stakeholder management
Authorize		Decision-making techniques	Decision-making approaches Optimization strategies
Reporting and Review	Reporting techniques Evaluation methodologies Communications skills	Meeting management Financial management	Communications management Stakeholder management Project audit methodologies
Strategic Change	Process improvement	Process development	Strategic planning Innovation management

Appendix G Portfolio Management Roles and Responsibilities

Portfolio	Identify	Categorize	Evaluate	Select	Prioritize	Balance	Authorize	Reporting and Review	Strategic Change
Review Board Members	Approve the portfolio management process	Approve the categorization process	Evaluate the performance of the portfolio and its components	Make decisions concerning components to pursue, defer, or terminate	Approve the prioritization process	Ensure that the priorities support the categorization	Allocate resources to components in the portfolio to be funded and continued according to business goals	Evaluate the effectiveness of the project portfolio management (PPM) process on a regularly scheduled basis to foster continuous improvements Provide ongoing oversight of the PPM process	Communicate strategic changes to the organization based on the portfolio's progress
Sponsors	Provide the business case for a portfolio component Champion the business case for the component								
Executive Managers	Serve as members of the Portfolio Review Board (PRB)					Communicate changes in strategic direction or marketplace developments	Reallaocate resources as required	Ensure goals of the portfolio are achieved	Validate the organization's strategic direction in light of PPM
Operations Managers	Provide information as requested to support the business case for a portfolio component	Provide information to the PPM manager as to categories for consideration in the PPM process	Provide information on resource availability		Provide information on any constraints that may affect the PPM process	Balance needs of ongoing processes with resources to support the projects and programs in the portfolio	Provide resources once the decision is made to authorize a new component in the portfolio	Provide data for the portfolio management information system Ensures resources are performing according to plan and are achieving strategic goals	Communicate strategic goals to the portfolio manager and the organization

Portfolio	Identify	Catagortize	Evaluate	Select	Prioritize	Balance	Authorize	Reporting and Review	Strategic Change
EPMO Director	Provides information as requested to support the business case for a portfolio component	Provides information to the Portfolio Manager as to categories for consideration in the PPM process	Provides information on resource availability Provides best practices on the performance of programs and projects		Provides information on any constraints that may affect the PPM process	Coordinates management of components under its area of responsibility	Provides resources once the decision is made to authorize a new component in the portfolio Reallocates resources as required based on decisions of the PRB and acquires resources if existing skills are insufficient	Ensures components are performing according to plan and are achieving strategic goals Takes preventive action as required Works with the Portfolio Manager to interface the PPM information system with the project management information system Conducts consistent reviews of the performance of programs and projects Provides data on the effectiveness of programs / projects in meeting cost, quality, and scope objectives	Participates in continuous improvement of the PPM process Identifies root causes if programs / projects are not meeting their strategic objectives and takes corrective action

Portfolio	Identify	Catagortize	Evaluate	Select	Prioritize	Balance	Authorize	Reporting and Review	Strategic Change
Program/Project Managers	Provides information as requested to support the business case for a portfolio component Work with sponsors to prepare the business case for a new component in the portfolio	Provides information to the Portfolio Manager as to categories for consideration in the PPM process Provide information to the Portfolio Manager as to categories for consideration in the PPM process	Provides information on resource availability		Provide information on any constraints that may affect the PPM process	Provide resources to assist in risk analysis as new components are being considered for authorization to the portfolio	Manage the budget/schedule of projects and programs and resources assigned to the projects and programs	Ensure resources are performing according to plan and are achieving strategic goals Manage ongoing program / project performance Provide data for the portfolio management information system Prepare recovery plans if projects / programs are in jeopardy of not achieving strategic goals Provide information concerning changes in project or program performance that may jeopardize progress	
Project Team Members	Work with sponsors to prepare the business case for a new component in the portfolio Provide information as requested to support the business case for a portfolio component						Complete deliverables as planned	Regularly report the status of assigned work to the project manager for data to be included in the portfolio management system	

Portfolio	Identify	Catagortize	Evaluate	Select	Prioritize	Balance	Authorize	Reporting and Review	Strategic Change
Functional Managers	Provide information as requested to support the business case for a portfolio component	Provide information to the Portfolio Manager as to categories for consideration in the PPM process	Provide information on resource availability		Provide information on any constraints that may affect the PPM process	Balance needs of ongoing functional responsibilities with resources to support the projects and programs in the portfolio	Provide resources once the decision is made to authorize a new component in the portfolio	Provide data for the portfolio management information system. Ensure resources are performing according to plan and are achieving strategic goals	
Finance Managers			Perform financial analysis information on components for use in the selection process			Provide budget information on components that may be authorized to be part of the portfolio. Work with the Portfolio Manager to interface the portfolio management information system with the financial and accounting systems		Monitor financial performance on components. Provide data for the portfolio management information system	Conduct regular reviews of the organization's competitive position in the marketplace

Appendix H

Work Breakdown Structure for the Project Portfolio Management System

1. Aligning
   a. Identification
      - Portfolio Component List
      - Component Categories
   b. Coordination
      - Component Decision Criteria
   c. Evaluation
      - Quantitative Indices/Models
      - Data Precision
      - Resource Availability
      - Key Performance Indicators
      - Portfolio Protocols
   d. Selection
      - Portfolio Recommendations
   e. Prioritization
      - Component Ranking
   f. Balancing
      - Strategic Alignment
      - Risk Management
   g. Authorization
      - Active Component Inventory
      - Budget Allocation

2. Monitoring and Controlling
   a. Reporting
      - Component Contributions
      - Key Performance Indicators
   b. Review
   c. Strategic Change
      - Benefit Contribution
   d. Portfolio Review Board Meetings

- Agenda
- Minutes and Action Items

e. Project Portfolio Management (PPM) Process
- Model Development
- Process Improvement Plan

f. PPM Information System
- Data Collection Process
- System Development
- System Implementation
- System Maintenance
- Interface to Other Information Systems

3. Project Management

a. Planning
- Project Charter
- Project Management Implementation Plan
- Project Work Breakdown Structure
- Project Scope Statement

b. Executing
- Things Issues
- People Issues
- Enterprise Issues
- Metrics

Appendix I

Project Portfolio Management Implementation Checklist

1. Manage the implementation of Project Portfolio Management just like that of a project
    a. Establish a vision for portfolio management in the organization
    b. Identify a sponsor for portfolio management
    c. Establish an integrated project team representing key areas of the business
        • Recognize that the team must be dedicated to the process
        • Ensure that team members are recognized contributors
        • Ensure that team members allocate needed time
    d. Have a kickoff meeting
    e. Assess the organization's maturity in portfolio management
    f. Collect baseline data:
        • How many programs/projects are under way?
        • How do these programs/projects match the strategic objectives?
        • How are programs/projects authorized today?
        • How is funding allocated?
        • How are resources allocated?
        • What are the interdependencies among programs/projects?
        • What types of data are collected on a routine basis?
        • What types of reviews are held?
        • Are projects ever cancelled?
        • How programs/projects are officially closed?
        • Is consistent information available across programs/projects?
        • Is an Enterprise Project Management Office in place?
        • What must be done to deliver the forecasted value according to the business operating plan?
        • Provide a report/presentation for executive management of both strengths and weaknesses.
    g. Prepare a charter for the Portfolio Manager
    h. Prepare a charter for the Portfolio Review Board (PRB)
    i. Determine roles and responsibilities for portfolio management in the organization

j. Appoint a Portfolio Manager and establish the PRB

k. Prepare a scope statement for portfolio management

l. Prepare a work breakdown structure for portfolio management

m. Prepare a portfolio management plan
- Describe objectives for portfolio management
- State milestones and completion targets
- Include a schedule
- Describe interfaces
- Provide a cost estimate

n. Conduct a stakeholder analysis
- Identify the key stakeholders
- Determine the key stakeholders' roles
- Prepare a stakeholder management plan

o. Prepare a communications management plan and distribute the portfolio management plan

p. Provide orientation sessions on portfolio management

q. Establish the portfolio management model to be used

r. Establish a portfolio management information system
- Determine data collection frequency
- Integrate this system with other systems in the organization

s. Establish a schedule of PRB meetings

t. Determine how reviews of the project portfolio management (PPM) process will be conducted to ascertain effectiveness

u. Update the PPM process as appropriate

v. Link PPM to the annual budgeting process

2. Actively manage the portfolio

a. Use the portfolio model

b. Set up a work authorization system

c. Conduct regular meetings of the PRB
- Distribute meeting results

d. Establish measures of success

e. Establish a survey of the effectiveness of the PPM process covering items such as satisfaction, quality, and value added, and conduct it at least on an annual basis

f. Continually review, reallocate, and update the PPM process

g. Establish a process to actively evaluate the effectiveness of the PPM process to ensure it has value

h. Document lessons learned

3. Recognize that PPM is a culture change

a. Ensure that people throughout the organization buy into the process

b. Recognize that people need to understand what is required

c. Conduct orientation sessions

d. Prepare an implementation plan

e. Provide training in portfolio management

f. Ensure continual affirmation of support for portfolio management by the sponsor

Appendix J

Communications Management Matrix

Key Stakeholders (Group or business unit)	Key messages to communicate (Purpose)	Communication methods to be used (Written, one-on-one, electronic, meetings, etc.)	Description of specific communications (Content, format, level of detail, etc.)	Timing/ Frequency (When, how often)
Portfolio Review Board	Component status	Written	Each component in the portfolio with a description of its status in priority order	Continuous update
	Meeting Information	Written	Schedule of upcoming meetings, agenda of upcoming meetings, minutes	Schedule—annually Agenda—one week before each meeting Minutes—day after meeting
	Action items	Electronic	Action items from previous meeting	Continuous Update
Program Managers	Resource issues

Programmatic performance issues | Progress meetings | Status / Progress Report | Monthly for meetings, weekly for reports |
| Project Managers | Project performance in terms of cost, scope, and schedule | Progress meetings | Status / Progress Report | Monthly for meetings, weekly for reports |
| Functional Managers | Overall staffing issues | Progress meetings | Resource histogram | Monthly for meetings, weekly for reports |

Appendix K

Proposal for a Project Portfolio Management Initiative Typical Contents

1. Portfolio Component Name
2. Component Description
   Purpose
   Problem to be Solved
   Overall Scope
   Exclusions
3. Component Category
4. Business Case
   Proposed Investment
   Estimated Total Project Cost
   Projected Return on Investment
   Estimated Business Value
   Estimated Schedule Duration
   Key Risks
   Key Issues
5. Key Constraints
6. Key Assumptions
7. Dependencies with Other Components
8. Required Resources
   Labor
       Required Areas of Expertise
       Number of People by Skill Type
   Materials
   Others

Appendix L

Project Portfolio Management Review Checklist

PORTFOLIO REVIEW BOARD MEETINGS
1. Are the Project Review Board (PRB) meetings held on a frequent basis?
2. Are the reviews focused on the portfolio as a whole, rather than only on a few projects?
3. Is the timing of the reviews predicated by organizational imperatives, rather than the status of individual projects?
4. Is a standard agenda used for PRB meetings?
5. Are minutes taken at each meeting and distributed to attendees?
6. Are action items from each meeting tracked until they are closed?
7. Do the PRB meetings result in decisions on the organization's project portfolio?
8. Are the decisions from the PRB meetings communicated throughout the organization?
9. Are decisions by the PRB made in a timely way?
10. If a Board member cannot attend a meeting, are substitute attendees for these Board members empowered to make decisions?
11. Do the PRB meetings include regular reviews of resource allocation and requirements to continue to support the current portfolio?
12. Do the PRB meetings result in changes such as:
    Postponing projects
    Terminating projects
    Realigning projects
13. Are status reports on each portfolio component provided to PRB members in advance of the meeting with significant information to enable them to be able to make decisions?
14. Do Board members share the rationale for making their decisions?
15. Are the PRB members selected on the basis of technical contributions?

PORTFOLIO MANAGEMENT PROCESS
1. Is the portfolio management process formalized?
2. Is the portfolio management process followed?
3. Is the portfolio management process considered an ongoing activity?

4. Is a collective portfolio in place with all the projects and programs undertaken by the organization?

5. Is the PPM process one that enables duplicate projects to be easily recognized?

6. Is a consistent, formalized ranking process used?

7. Are standard templates used to:

    Submit projects for consideration?

    Document decisions that are made by the PRB?

8. Is the process to proportion funding among project types in the organization documented?

9. Is the process to submit new projects/programs to the portfolio straightforward?

10. Is each project evaluated as to its:

    Complexity

    Resource requirements

    Contribution to strategic goals

    Risks

    Constraints

11. Does the stage-gate process add value?

12. Are the thresholds for tolerance for deviations from plans appropriate?

13. Do the components in the portfolio support the organization's vision and strategic goals?

14. Is each component tracked on a regular basis?

15. Is the PPM process reviewed periodically to determine whether changes are required?

16. Are resource estimates updated as required?

17. Is the portfolio balanced so that it optimizes business value?

18. Are risks for each project assessed prior to their inclusion in the portfolio?

19. Are actual project outcomes tracked against the proposed targets?

20. Are interdependencies between portfolio components known and managed?

PORTFOLIO MANAGEMENT MODEL

1. Does the model make a distinction between organizational issues and project issues?

2. Does the model make a distinction between strategic issues and financial issues?

3. Does the model have the capability to rank many projects at one time?

4. Does the model enable the opportunity to give more importance to some features than others?

5. Does the model include all of the organizational objectives of a PPM system?

6. Can the model compare projects of different disciplines?

7. Can the model handle all projects in one collective portfolio?

8. Is the model updated periodically?

9. Is there a process in place for reviewing and modifying the model in the light of changes in organizational environment?

10. Is the model easily understandable?

PORTFOLIO MANAGEMENT INFORMATION SYSTEM

1. Is the portfolio management information system easy to use?

2. Are data in the system timely regarding:

Objectives

Cost

Resources

Schedule

Deliverables

3. Does the portfolio management information system provide the data that are needed to:

Assess the status of the portfolio?

Determine each project's contribution to the portfolio?

Determine each project's status within the portfolio?

Analyze the organization's resources and how they are allocated across portfolio components?

Track any trends in the portfolio?

Anticipate issues that will require resolution?

4. Does the portfolio management information system contain data on all of the projects under way in the organization?

5. Is the system integrated with related information systems in the organization?

Project management

Human resource management

Business development/opportunity management
Financial management/accounting
6. Is the system an integrated decision-making tool so that it can use the progress of the project along with its budgeted scope-cost-duration attributes to determine whether or not a project should go forward?
7. Is a digital dashboard available to show all the projects in the portfolio and their status?
8. Are exception reports provided as requested in a timely way?
9. Does the information system provide tools to summarize and analyze the raw data?
10. Are the data in the system available to everyone?

PORTFOLIO MANAGER AND STAFF
1. Does the Portfolio Manager report at a significant level in the organization to effect change?
2. Does the Portfolio Manager and/or staff monitor projects in light of:
Evolving corporate strategy
Individual project performance
Overall enterprise resource demands
3. Are there competency standards for the portfolio manager?
4. Are there competency standards for a portfolio team member?
5. Is the portfolio team as a whole empowered to make preliminary analyses and determinations regarding pursuit or termination of portfolio components?

ROLES AND RESPONSIBILITIES
1. Is the portfolio management structure formalized in the organization?
2. Do the various participants in the PPM process understand their roles and responsibilities?
3. Are sponsors and program/project managers held accountable for the results?
4. Is open communication the norm among participants in the PPM process?
5. Does the PPM process provide motivation to project and program managers to enhance the quality of the information available on their projects and programs so that better decisions can be made?

VALUE OF PROJECT PORTFOLIO MANAGEMENT

1. Do people throughout the organization recognize the value of portfolio management and the importance of PPM to the organization?
2. Have orientation sessions on portfolio management been conducted?
3. Have program and project managers received training in the PPM process?
4. Is a method in place to measure the value of portfolio management to the organization?
5. Is the portfolio management function considered an ongoing process?

4. A Comprehensive Project Portfolio Management Model

A portfolio management system is considered a success if it routinely selects the right projects and abandons the inappropriate projects. Such repeatable performance must be based on a methodical set of procedures and tools that represent an organizational culture that is conducive to project management success. The project portfolio management (PPM) system must have the support of a fully functional Enterprise Project Management Office (EPMO), which, in turn, must have the real and committed support of the upper management of the organization.

A successful PPM system is one that engages corporate leadership in developing the guidelines and standards for the management of portfolios of projects. With all selection and management criteria explicitly outlined, a team other than upper management can manage the portfolio in a straightforward fashion. However, in the absence of a fully formalized set of guidelines, PPM should involve upper management in the regular process of selecting and prioritizing projects. Therefore, the existence of a quantitative model of any sophistication is an indication that the organization is on its path toward a formalized prioritization process.

A fully functional EPMO will compile and distribute the best practices of project management to the entire organization. In turn, the teams will adhere to those guidelines as a consistent method of achieving success in all activities of project management, program management, and portfolio management. By definition, these guidelines will cover things issues, people issues, and enterprise issues. (Figure 1)

One of the basic symptoms of the sophistication of the organization is the existence, or lack thereof, of an organizational unit that promotes unified PPM activities. This unit is commonly known as the EPMO. Regardless of what this organizational entity is called, the texture and intensity of its functions will signal the overall project management health of the organization.

If the bulk of the effort of the EPMO is spent in augmenting, mentoring, and consulting functions, it is very likely that the organization is in its infancy with respect to PPM, program management, or even in single-project management. In such a case, portfolios, programs, and even projects, typically do not conduct

Figure 1

their missions successfully. If there is no concerted effort to change these circumstances toward repeatable success, that would be a signal that the upper management of the organization is comfortable with the existing inefficiencies. At the other end of the spectrum, if the organization has a fully functional EPMO, portfolios of projects, programs, and individual projects should always be successful. One would hope that success is always noticed and often celebrated, which in turn might perpetuate future success. (Figure 2).

Ideally, the vast majority of PPM duties should be conducted by a portfolio management team and guided by the enterprise-oriented functions of the EPMO. In such a case, the PPM system will benefit substantially and significantly from the facilitative foundations provided by the enterprise-oriented functions of the EPMO, namely: practice, act as a clearinghouse, promote, and train. However, it is entirely possible that, even in partly mature organizations, the EPMO might provide most of the enterprise-oriented functions but also a small amount of team-focused functions, namely: augment, consult, and mentor. Thus, even if the organization is mature in most processes dealing with management of individual projects, the EPMO would assign personnel to assist upper management in conducting debates and facilitating

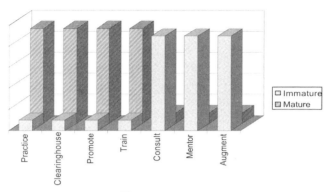

Figure 2

decisions to prioritize projects and assign resources to authorized projects.

Given that the portfolio management system would handle very large sums of the corporation's funds, it must be highly comprehensive. Even though variations of the same model might be used to prioritize different groups of projects, there should be a collective portfolio containing all of the projects undertaken by the entire organization. Additionally, the portfolio evaluation system should be sophisticated enough to recognize duplicate projects so that a decision can be made to combine them. Independent of how the data on deliverable attributes are created and ranked, best results can be achieved if the projects are ranked using a consistent tool and formalized process, as frequently as possible, throughout the life of all projects.

Current portfolio management models refer to a large number of project attributes and organizational attributes, during the process of arriving at a prioritized list of projects. Sometimes these attributes are expressed numerically, and sometimes they are expressed verbally. The first step in formalizing the PPM process is to develop a numeric value, or an index, for incorporation into an explicit and quantitative model. Naturally, the extent to which the model includes quantified descriptions of all pertinent issues is an indication of the organization's maturity. Quantifying all the attributes, and incorporating the indices into a unified model, has the subtle advantage of facilitating the articulation of all the issues that are important to the organization. Additionally, quantified attributes, or indices, promote a uniform decision-making process, thus adding a certain level of consistency to the prioritization process. With these indices in place, the organization can move on to creating a model. When the model is in place, the organization can then establish a uniform review cycle for projects.

The indices that comprise a portfolio management model can be divided into two distinct categories: those that deal with the attributes and goals of the sponsoring organization, and those that deal with the features of the projects that are intended to meet the identified organizational goals. The category of indices that characterize the organizational goals includes those indices focusing on business objectives, strategy, profitability, market conditions, interest rates, and general economic growth. The organizational-related indices can be either quantitative or qualitative. Quantitative indices are usually finance-based, have a definite formula, and are relatively easy to determine. Qualitative indices are usually rooted in strategy, competitiveness, or marketability. Qualitative organizational indices tend to be more experience-based and subjective. The category of indices that characterize the project includes ones that deal with performance, or predicted performance, of individual projects, specifically cost, schedule, and deliverable.

This book advocates a distinction between the indices that describe the deliverable and indices that describe the organizational business case that created the project and will ultimately benefit from the project deliverable. To carry that one step further, it also is useful to distinguish between financial and strategic indices that are evaluated as part of the project prioritization process.

4.1 Project-Related Indices

The first time that the project is submitted for evaluation and possible adoption, the project attributes can only be described in broad terms. However, some time after the project is selected for implementation, the data will be somewhat accurate and precise during the first few evaluations of the portfolio, one of which is this specific project. Finally, as the portfolio, and this specific project as part of it, is evaluated during the latter stages of the project, the data, hopefully, are exceptionally detailed and accurate. (Figure 3)

The accuracy of the project information might be anywhere from very rough to very precise, depending on when the deliverable information was generated, and the amount of definitive information available about the project. Thus, the portfolio decisions made on the basis of rough estimates will also carry the same level of inaccuracy, which is why the portfolio

● ◉ ◉ | # Project Attributes

- ○ Cost
  - ◉ Conceptual for Authorization
  - ◉ Semi-detailed for Continuation
  - ◉ Detailed for Re-evaluation
- ○ Duration
  - ◉ Initial for Authorization
  - ◉ Semi-detailed for Continuation
  - ◉ Detailed for Re-evaluation
- ○ Scope and Quality
  - ◉ General for Authorization
  - ◉ Semi-Focused for Continuation
  - ◉ Sharply Focused for Re-evaluation

Figure 3

decision will have to be revisited as more accurate project information becomes available. In a way, the process of initial prioritization, which is based on rough order-of-magnitude estimates of cost and schedule, can be regarded as a qualitative-based process, because it is not detailed and does not lend itself to much quantification. On the other hand, midstream evaluations can and must be quantitative-based and far more definitive.

As a barometer of how well the company handles PPM, it would be informative to look through the project records and determine how the project progress is normally reported for the projects of the portfolio, and how many times the progress of each project is viewed in light of the portfolio constraints. If the organization does not keep detailed project records of this analysis, then the organization is missing one of the major components of portfolio management, which is the formalized management of the projects and the resulting value of historical information for future projects. These are also clearly the symptoms of an immature organization.

4.2 Enterprise-Related Indices

The organizational attributes of the project do not necessarily describe the project; rather, they describe the needs and imperatives of the organization that will justify the funding of the project. These needs and strategic directives will determine the way the project attributes will be judged during the midstream project portfolio prioritization reviews. The business case or vision of

Organizational Attributes That Temper Project Prioritization

- o Financial
  - Return on Investment
  - Payback Period
- o Strategic
  - Competitive Edge
  - Time to Market
  - Utility
- o Funding Category Constraints
  - Funding Proportion within Each Portfolio
  - Project Population Distribution within Each Portfolio
  - Continuous Pipeline Delivery within Each Portfolio

Figure 4

the project should be a definitive description independent of the conceptual data that describe the deliverable. Although many organizations use enterprise-related indices in selecting projects, such a selection process is highly debate-oriented, is based primarily on verbal descriptions, and usually is not based on quantified characterizations.

The organizational attributes might describe three separate issues: financial, strategic, or funding groups (Figure 4).

The financial indices will focus on a project in isolation of other issues, in that financial indices test whether or not in the long run this project will be self-supporting and self-sustaining. The strategic indices describe the general direction of the organization and the extent to which that direction translates into funding for the various initiatives. The strategic indices will always be influenced by external factors such as the status of the overall economic climate, the sophistication of the competition, and the changes in the clients' strategic directions. Funding group constraints reflect a slightly different facet of business and strategic requirements. The three most common categories of constraints are funding proportion, population distribution, and pipeline issues. The funding proportion constraint will prescribe that the funding for a specific group cannot be less/more than a pre-designated percentage of the overall funds. The population distribution constraint will prescribe that, at any given time and independent of the cost of the projects, the number of projects in a given group cannot be more/less than a pre-designated number. Finally, the pipeline issues will prescribe that, independent of other considerations, there should be enough projects in the execution pipeline such that the deliverables for those projects will be completed at a pre-designated pace, for example, every quarter, every six months, every year, etc.

Given that organizational indices reflect the current status of the organization, their description and accurate quantification should be always available. For example, the return on investment (ROI) requirements, and the way projects would be measured on that basis, should always be explicitly and formally available. Thus, probably there will not be a distinction between the values of the indices that describe the financial, strategic, and funding category characteristics of an organization, whether they are used for the original prioritization, or if they are used for the midstream prioritization. By contrast, the accuracy of the deliverable-related indices will change throughout the life of the project.

The resources that are available for projects will influence the organization's overall philosophy in managing projects because resources must be available to implement both the current and forecasted projects. If the organizational project management maturity is at the higher end of the maturity scale, then there is a clear picture of the number of resources that are available, and there is a realistic expectation of how many projects the resource pool can support. Thus, given these desirable circumstances, the organization can actively practice the management-by-projects concept.

4.2.1 Financial and Strategic Factors Influencing Portfolios

The enterprise-related indices that are normally used to measure and evaluate the projects within the portfolio are usually derived either from financial factors or from strategic factors. Indices derived from financial factors are usually quantitative, whereas indices derived from strategic factors are usually qualitative.

Financial indices are by far the most frequently used indices in portfolio management, partly because in the eyes of upper management they have a ring of familiarity to them, and partly because they are significantly easier to quantify and calculate (Figure 5).

By comparison, strategic indices are highly qualitative, and sometimes, they defy quantification. Notwithstanding, there has been some effort in quantifying the strategic issues. Such quantification will require a predeter-

● ● ● | **Organizational Indices That Determine the Financial Attractiveness of the Investment**

- Internal Rate of Return
- Net Present Value of Earnings
- Benefit/Cost Ratio
- Expected Commercialization Value
- Time to Breakeven
- Discounted Cash Flow of the Income from the Deliverable
- Total Cost as a Percentage of the Total Available Funds
- Relationship to the Total Expected Value of the Portfolio

Figure 5

mined scale and a set of guidelines as to how to rate the strategic indices that point to the business cases of individual projects.

The strategic goal of an organization is one of the most illusive concepts, certainly in the context of a project portfolio model, primarily because it does not lend itself to easy definition and/or quantification. Notwithstanding, often the upper management might be comfortable in knowing exactly what it is and/or might be able to provide a narrative definition for it. Consequently, there are usually numerous ways of verbally describing a particular organizational strategy. Probably the most accurate way of describing the strategic direction is, not necessarily to recite the idealized descriptor of the vision and goals, but rather, to develop a distillation of the initiatives for the projects that are currently underway, and recently completed, within the organization.

Figure 6 presents an example of some organizational indices that may be used. This includes areas such as increasing the organization's competitive edge, its time to market, product innovation, overall customer satisfaction, support of current and future customer needs, improving relationships with stake holders, social responsibility, flexibility, and productivity.

Figure 7 shows examples of how strategic indices can be quantified for use in the prioritization models. This figure shows examples of the kind of scales that can be developed to assist with developing numeric ratings from narrative plateaus for the seemingly qualitative issues of new business marketability, cost savings, and profitability. Naturally, the assignment of scales to narrative descriptors of enterprise issues will be organization specific and

Organizational Indices That Determine the Strategic Attractiveness of the Deliverable

- o Benefits of the deliverable to the Enterprise
  - Morale
  - Prestige
  - Customer relations
  - Productivity
- o Strategic Importance
- o Utility of the Deliverable
- o Probability of Success of the Business Venture Using the Deliverable

Figure 6

might even change with time as the organization modifies its strategic and financial objectives. It is an important point that quantitative indices will enable the enterprise executives to consider more important long-term issues such as continuous improvement, rather than focusing only on short-term single project success.

Rating Guideline Examples

- o **New Business – Is this project outside of our current operational norm?**
  - 100% new business   Score of 10
  - 50% new business and 50% baseline   Score of 8
  - – Typical project, current technology   Score of 5

- o **Marketability – Can this solution be used in other organizational units?**
  - Project solution transferable   Score of 10
  - Limited to this client only   Score of 5

- o **Cost Savings - This project is expected to have operational savings of :**
  - In excess of 20 %   Score of 10
  - Between 15% to 20%   Score of 8
  - Between 10% to 15%   Score of 7
  - Breakeven   Score of 5

- o **Profitability – This project will impact the organizational profit margin**
  - Exceeds the norm by 20% or more.   Score of 10
  - Exceeds the norm by 10% to 20%.   Score of 8
  - Meets the norm   Score of 5
  - At Breakeven   Score of 0

Figure 7

4.2.2 Funding Groups

One of the constraints of a project portfolio is the annual budget that is available to the portfolio. The annual budget must be judiciously dispersed among authorized projects. Given that portfolio funds are hardly ever limitless, it is this financial restriction that, when it is trickled down, will be manifested in a shortage of cash flow, or a shortage of resources, during a given time frame, which, in turn, will cause an expansion of the duration of some of the projects or the cancellation of some of the projects. The funding group schema is used as the first step in the distribution of the organizational funds to projects in that each group is allocated a certain amount of annual or total project funds. The funding group indices are probably the most illusive of the three sets of organizational attributes that describe a project, the three attributes being strategic attractiveness, financial viability, and funding group imperatives. Thus, the impact of the funding group imperatives on the project selection process often appears to be arbitrary or, at least, judgment based. The funding group indices can be in one of three separate forms: by total number of projects, by funding percentage, or by pipeline population (Figure 8).

Depending on the operational focus of the organization, the grouping of projects can be by number of projects in each funding group. This schema is used when there might be a necessity, or a desire, for a minimum or a maximum number of projects in a given funding group. This method is used primarily in cases where projects are people-intensive, and the enterprise would like to productively employ all of its people resources, while allowing all areas some benefit from the, admittedly, limited resources.

Funding Group Constraints

- Minimum or Maximum Number of Projects in each Group
- Minimum or Maximum Percentage of Project Funds in Relation to the Total Group Funds
- Continuous Delivery of Projects in each Group
  - Pipeline Population Issues
  - Staggered Delivery Dates

Figure 8

Alternately, the categorization can be by total cost of all projects in each funding group. This schema is used when there is a necessity, or a desire, for a minimum or maximum percentage of the portfolio funds to be allocated to a certain funding group. This method is used when total project cost is an issue, but cost and availability of project people are not a concern. An example of such a case is when projects are not people intensive, but instead are equipment intensive, or when projects are dependent on a limited infrastructure.

The third schema for categorization is by delivery date, in cases where the most important requirement is to have a new product every period. There might be a necessity that at any given time there must be a minimum or maximum number of projects from each group in the portfolio, or that there must be sufficient numbers of projects of a given funding group in the portfolio such that the product pipeline results in a new product at a given cycle time. This is applicable to most industries where new products and new features give the enterprise a competitive edge. Examples of these cases are the pharmaceutical, automotive, electronic, and software industries where the new product pipeline should always be full by any means possible.

The most commonly used basis of categorization is to assign funding percentages or funding amounts to various project groupings. A variety of schemas can be used to develop a percentile funding structure. One of the traditional schemas for grouping projects, for accounting or for evaluation purposes, is by functional or divisional designations. Thus, they would be grouped into operational, maintenance, etc. Alternately, projects can be divided into financially identifiable groups such as high risk, low cost, etc. Other times, projects are grouped by specialty areas that they aim to support and/or by the specialty areas where they are intended to provide capability improvement. Examples of this latter grouping are wires, servers, transmission protocols, and in other industries, they can be heart disorders, blood disorders, orthopedic health, etc. (Figure 9).

Figure 10 shows a typical categorization nomenclature based on financial and strategic categories, whereas Figure 11 shows a categorization based on capability improvement specialty areas. The distinction between these two types of categories is that the former groups the projects by their strategic and financial attributes, whereas the latter groups the projects by the specialty area of capability improvement or research. Strategic and financial groups tend to be generic and all encompassing, whereas capability improvement or research groups are usually specific in nature and refer to a unique technical specialty.

Portfolio Groups

o Divisional Categories
  - Operational
  - Maintenance

o Strategic or Financial Categories
  - High Risk
  - High Payout
  - Low Cost

o Capability Improvement, or Research Topic, Categories
  - Wires
  - Servers
  - Mechanical Engineering
  - Heart Disorders

Figure 9

Strategic and Financial Funding Groups

o Risk
  - High Risk, High Reward
  - High Risk, Low Reward
  - Low Risk, High Reward
  - Low Risk, Low Reward
o Urgency of Deliverable
  - Shortage or Overage of Resources
  - Operational Necessity
  - Long-Term Payoff
  - Competitive Positioning

Figure 10

Figure 12 shows a sample of funding distribution among categories, in a case where arbitrarily a fixed percentage of funds has been allocated to each of these categories. In this case, the projects within each funding group compete for funds only with projects in that funding group and not across the larger portfolio that includes all of the projects.

Figure 13 depicts a typical project disposition chart, which would be the ultimate result of a prioritization exercise. This chart shows the distinct capability improvement areas which constitute the portfolio groupings. Within each group, projects are listed according to their ranking derived from the prioritization model. The implication is that projects higher on the list in each funding

Capability Improvement or Research Funding Groups

o Network Connection Issues
o Mechanical Devices
o Blood Disorders
o Heart Disease
o Heart Ailments

Figure 11

group will receive funding until such point that all of the funds in that funding group have been allocated. Therefore, the execution or continuation of projects in each category, represented by its separate column, will be authorized down to the point that the funds in that category are depleted.

Divisional Funding Groups Project Funding Distribution

o Information Systems	10%
o New Facilities	20%
o Applied Research	20%
o New Products	15%
o New Line of Business	20%
o Enhance Intellectual Capital	15%

Figure 12

Independent of what prioritization schema is used, a formalized prioritization process provides enough data so that one can visually examine the current relative funding weight of each funding group, such as what is shown in Figure 14.

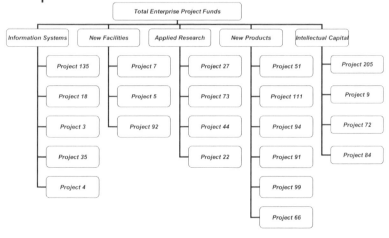

Figure 13

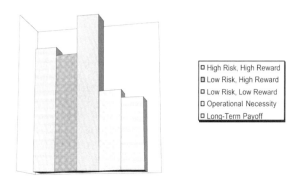

Figure 14

To carry that further, one can also review the strategic transformation of the organization, as manifested by funding allocations among different funding groups during a multi-year period. (Figure 15) Such a historical chart is an accurate barometer of the most recent past and current strategic direction of the organization. Therefore, it is a realistic view of the project investment patterns of the organization. For example, the illustrative example indicates that high-risk and long-term categories have gone through a funding peak during the previous year. One would hope that the investment pattern in these areas has been deliberate and is not accidental.

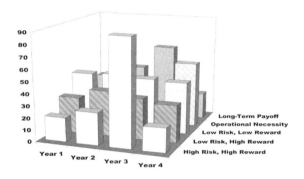

Figure 15

Funding group indices are complex and will continue to be determined through debate, judgment, and verbal comparison. Refinements and enhancement of these indices and their associated schemas would probably become the next phase of implementation of formalized PPM systems. A starting point for comparing and prioritizing funding groups would be a structure similar to the one shown in Figure 16, where an example of prioritizing across funding groups would be that the proportion of funds allocated to these three groups would be based on the scores that the projects in the group earn from number of projects, funding proportion, and pipeline population. Using this example, the authorization of projects in a portfolio could be influenced by how many projects are currently in that group, what percentage of corporate funds this group currently consumes, and how regularly the deliverables of the projects of this portfolio will be released to the organization for the foreseeable future. For example, the organizational policies could require that the importance to these three grouping imperatives be quantified at 2, 2, and 6, respectively. Such a circumstance would signal the notion that it is far more important that the delivery pipeline for that particular group result in new products, than it is for the group to spend a certain amount of resources, or that there be a certain number of ongoing projects in that group.

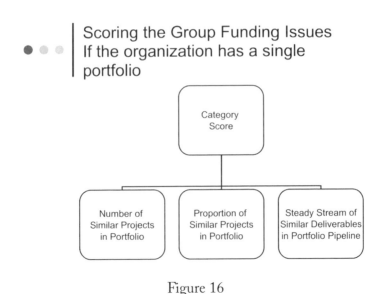

Figure 16

4.3 Portfolio Prioritization Model

The current portfolio management models tend to be mostly qualitative and judgment based. Even those that are quantitative tend not to be mathematically complex, albeit, many are regarded as effective and satisfactory by their respective enterprises. The structure described in this chapter is an initial attempt at putting a formality and directness into the process, by way of quantifying all indices, and by way of providing a mechanism to explicitly state the relative importance of portfolio management indices. The structure used in this model follows the well-known Work Breakdown Structure (WBS).

Using this structure for the characterization and calculation of a project scoring indicator, the first level of this structure will have elements for project attributes and enterprise attributes. (Figure 17)

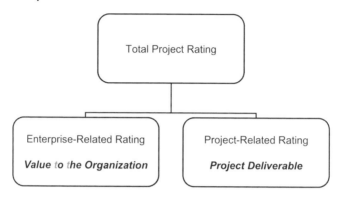

Project Rating Attributes for Prioritization Model

Total Project Rating

Enterprise-Related Rating

Value to the Organization

Project-Related Rating

Project Deliverable

Figure 17

The relative weight placed on each of the elements of this structure will depend on organizational objectives, strategic goals, and the corporate environment. For example, the index describing the cost/schedule attributes of the project deliverable could be only half as important as the value of the deliverable to the organization. That would give rise to the situations where a large amount of cost overruns and schedule delays will be deliberately tolerated because the deliverable is more important to the organization than is the cost.

Figure 18 shows a slightly more complex expansion of this model, suitable for evaluation of projects within a certain funding group.

In this model, the enterprise issues, or the value to the organization, are explicitly divided into financial and strategic, and the indices within each group are enumerated. Using this model, projects of the same funding group can be compared and prioritized. Through such an approach, the project portfolio team has the tool to assign different degrees of importance to the project deliverable, the strategic importance of the deliverable, and the financial implications of the revenues of the project. To carry that one step further, one can assign different degrees of importance to cost, duration, ROI, and competitive issues of the project deliverable. Figure 19 shows the assignment of points to each of these indices.

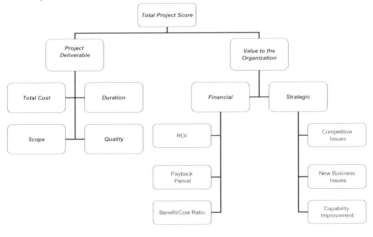

Figure 18

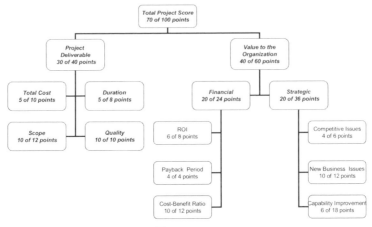

Figure 19

In this example, the total number of possible points that a project can achieve is 100. For the purposes of this illustration, the indices of importance have been determined to be those listed on the model, albeit, the list of indices is expected to be different for each organization, in line with that organization's strategic missions. On the basis of the objectives of the

mythical organization illustrated here, the individual indices have been assigned points whose total is 100. As is shown on this illustration, the project deliverable has a weight of 40 points, while the value to the organization has a combined weight of 60. These scoring points are quantitative
indications of the importance of each particular index to the organization.
It is a significant issue that another organization might assign entirely different points to their indices, even if the organization uses the same suite
of indices. The project shown in this example scored 30/40 points for
the attributes of the deliverable, 20/24 points for the strategic importance of
its deliverable, and 20/36 points for the financial implications of the project
deliverable. Thus, the total score for this project is 70/100.

Alternately, the prioritization model could be constructed such that all
of the indices of the model have the same importance, and therefore, they all
have the same weight. Thus, the total score for a project is determined by a
simple addition of the rating values of the constituent indices of this model.
The individual ratings for the constituent elements are all on a scale of one
to ten. A mythical project in this mythical organization might rate 57 points
with this model, based on how the various indices were rated for that project
(Figure 20). It is an important point that the absolute value of the total score
of the project is not nearly as important as the relative values calculated for
each of the projects within the portfolio.

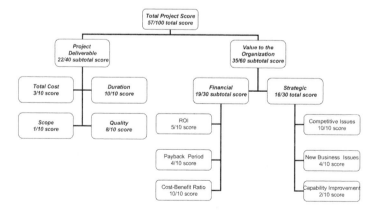

Figure 20

A level of sophistication can be added to this basic model by assigning weights to the level one elements of this model. (Figure 21) Under this schema, the values of the indices within the deliverable category, financial category, and strategic category will continue to be linearly added. Each index is rated on a scale of 10, and the results of the lower-level elements are added through a simple addition. Thus, the total score for the deliverable, financial, and strategic elements of this model are 22, 19, and 16, respectively. The blending of financial and strategic categories, in order to arrive at the value to the organization index, will be accomplished by assigning weights of 7 and 9 to the financial and strategic categories, respectively. The values of 7 and 9

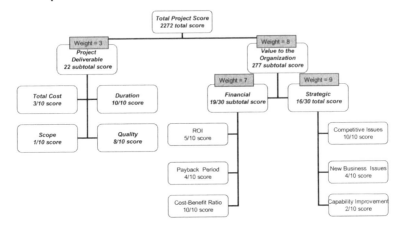

Figure 21

are numbers assigned arbitrarily to signify the relative importance of financial and strategic issues. Thus, the organizational score, as derived from financial and strategic scores, will be 7x19+9x16=277. Finally, the overall rating will be achieved by using the weights and ratings of the project and organizational blocks. Therefore, the project and organizational scores of 22 and 277 will result in a total score of 2,282, when they are combined with their weight of 3 and 8, respectively, before summing the two. Again, the total score for one project will not be as significant as the comparison of the scores of two projects of the portfolio with the use of the same schema.

Another level of formalized sophistication can be added to this model by calculating percentages for each of the three top-level elements: project, financial, and strategic. For simplicity of illustration, the project and value to the organization indices are derived by simple addition of their sub-elements. Thus, the linear scoring of the deliverable is 30/40 or 75%. Likewise, the linear scoring of the value to the organizational issues is 40/60 or 66%. Then, the next step would be to multiply these percentages to arrive at the percent rating of the project or 49.5%. This percentage can now be used to compare several projects among one another (Figure 22). Although in this illustration the top-level score is derived through a multiplier schema, the score for the bottom branch scores are derived through linear addition. One can choose to use a multiplier schema even for the component elements of each branch. In such a case, the total score for the deliverable would be derived by multiplying the percentage score for its components, namely cost, scope, duration, and quality. Likewise, the organization score will be derived from multiplying the financial and strategic percentages, while each of those percentages is derived from multiplying the scores of their respective components.

Project Scoring Model
Multiplier Schema

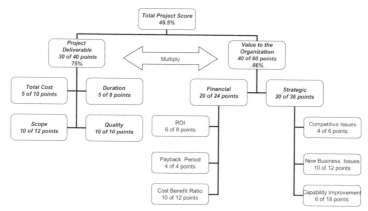

Figure 22

4.4 The Review Cycle

The PPM cycle is a repeating cycle New projects are periodically added to the portfolio and some of the existing projects are removed from the portfolio (Figure 23). There are two modes by which projects are removed from the portfolio. One is the joyous case in which the project delivers its intended product and is formally closed. The other is the somewhat difficult case where

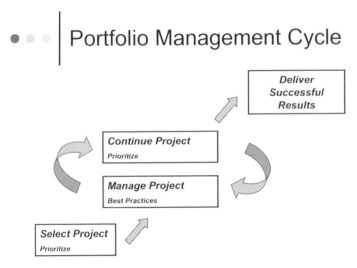

Figure 23

either the project is considered out of control, or, even in the case of a smooth running project, it is determined that the product is no longer needed (Figure 24). Understandably, removal of projects from the portfolio is very rare in organizations that do not have a formal portfolio structure and in organizations where a methodical evaluation is non-existent.

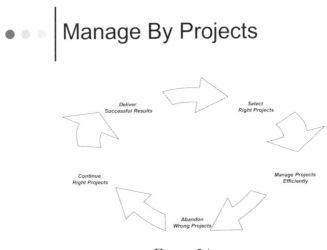

Figure 24

The portfolio management cycle will start with selecting projects for execution through the use of formalized and sophisticated portfolio management tools and processes. The accuracy of the results of this phase will depend on the quality of the portfolio model and the procedures employed while using that model. The next phase of this cycle will involve managing the projects, programs, and portfolios of the organization using formalized project management tools, techniques, and processes. It is this phase of the cycle that would depend on the competency of the project teams to deliver the projects in the shortest amount of time, with the lowest cost and at the highest quality. The next phase of this cycle is essentially a reiteration of the first phase in which projects that are new to the portfolio, and projects that are existing in the portfolio, are matched against each other, against newly proposed projects, and against the current articulation of the organizational strategies and goals (Figure 25). As part of this evaluation, some new projects will be added to the portfolio, some of the existing projects will be continued, and some of the existing projects will be terminated.

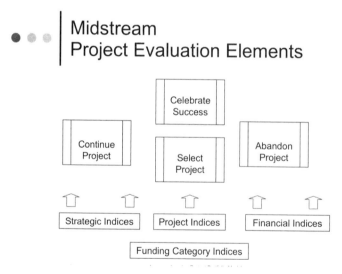

Figure 25

Those indices that describe the project, such as cost, schedule, and scope, are very sketchy during the early stages of the project's life cycle and during the first few cycles that the project is introduced into the portfolio. However, as the project progresses through its phases, this information will become increasingly more accurate (Figure 26).

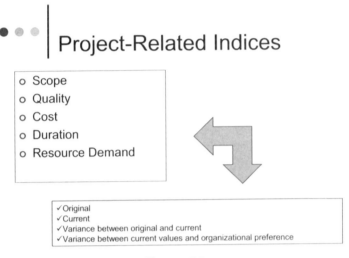

Project-Related Indices

o Scope
o Quality
o Cost
o Duration
o Resource Demand

✓ Original
✓ Current
✓ Variance between original and current
✓ Variance between current values and organizational preference

Figure 26

Thus, beyond measuring the basic attributes of cost, schedule, and scope, it would be informative to measure and report the variance of their current values as they are compared against their respective original values. If the organization is sophisticated in project management, and thus has a wealth of historical data and planning tools, the variances would be predictable and/or small. Notwithstanding the accuracy and predictability of the project indices, the review process might choose to assign importance to the variances in the value of the indices that signify the project deliverable. The variances can be computed in comparison with each index's original value and/or the current organizational tolerance for that index.

On the other hand, there is no rational reason why the enterprise-related indices should not be accurate at all times. An enlightened and methodical organization should be able to quantify, or at least definitively describe, the organizational issues that create the projects, justify their funding, and ultimately will benefit from the deliverables of those projects. The enterprise-related indices would quantitatively characterize strategic issues, financial issues, and funding group imperatives (Figure 27). Admittedly, these are the indices that defy quantification, which is why they have traditionally been described verbally. However, a methodical management of the portfolio of projects would require quantification of these indices and a continual update of those quantified values in concert with the organization's evolving circumstances.

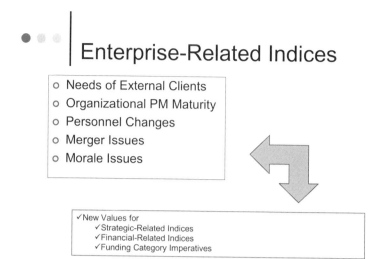

Enterprise-Related Indices

o Needs of External Clients
o Organizational PM Maturity
o Personnel Changes
o Merger Issues
o Morale Issues

✓New Values for
   ✓Strategic-Related Indices
   ✓Financial-Related Indices
   ✓Funding Category Imperatives

Figure 27

The portfolio management team should have the most current prioritization models at its disposal every time it reviews the projects of the portfolio. The portfolio team should also have current values for the weights of the various indices of the models that will be used (Figure 28). Finally, the portfolio team must have a set of up-to-date data for the project's deliverable and for the project team's success in meeting the targets of that deliverable.

Portfolio Management
Progression of Evaluation Data

o **Updated Models for**
   ○ Project Attributes
   ○ Funding Structure
   ○ Strategic-Related Indices
   ○ Financial-Related Indices

o **Current Values for**
   ○ Funding Groups
   ○ Strategic-Related Indices
   ○ Financial-Related Indices

o **Enhanced Predictions for the Project's**
   ○ Cost
   ○ Duration
   ○ Scope
   ○ Quality

Figure 28

4.5 Monitoring Projects in the Portfolio

Once the projects have been properly selected and prioritized, the remaining tasks of a well-run PPM system include methodically managing portfolios of projects from a unified funding structure, carefully managing multiple projects from a single resource pool, and properly managing individual projects to their respective point of successful completion.

Ultimately, the success of the project is measured in how well the team handles the things issues such as cost, schedule, and scope. Admittedly, things issues are often influenced by people and enterprise issues. To carry this point further, there are four areas of knowledge in which the project team must be conversant as part of their daily activities: technical specialty of the project, managing project things, managing project people, and managing enterprise issues. (Figure 29) A sophisticated team will deal with all of them, while an unsophisticated team will focus on only the things issues. The extent to which the project team successfully deals with more than one of these issues is an indirect indication of team maturity. If the team is a typical team of the organization, then this rough indicator of the maturity of the team will provide an inference for the organizational maturity.

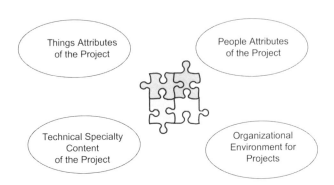

Figure 29

As the team strives to deliver the project in line with client expectations for cost-schedule-scope, and as the team handles the subordinate issues such as contracts and risks, the team will also need to deal with the people issues of the project. The people issues can arise from interactions of people within the team, between the team and the client, and between the team and other stakeholders (Figure 30). Finally, the team must be mindful of those relationships that do not impact the project at hand but that will influence the general project management culture of the organization and success of future projects. These issues usually arise when the lessons-learned point to changes in the approval cycle, and the execution style, for future projects. To some extent, there is a relationship between success in managing project issues and success in managing organizational issues, because measuring success in project issues measures success of the project itself, and measuring success in managing enterprise issues measures the friendliness of the infrastructure for that success.

Project Performance Issues

- o Cost
- o Schedule
- o Scope and Quality
- o People Issues
  - Within the Team
  - Between the Team and the Client
  - Between the Team and Stakeholders
  - Peripheral Relationships

Figure 30

For uniformity of performance, and just so that the experience of successful project teams is continually transferred to everyone within the organization, there must be procedures and guidelines for all of the activities of the project team. Project success is repeatable and predictable when all project teams follow these guidelines and experience success with these guidelines (Figure 31). The team must be conversant and competent in all project management knowledge areas such as cost, schedule, risk, etc. To assist the team members in carrying out their duties expeditiously and successfully, the organization must provide uniform procedures and guidelines as to the proper handling of these issues. Additionally, there must be sufficient evidence that following these guidelines will result in predictable success.

Individual Projects

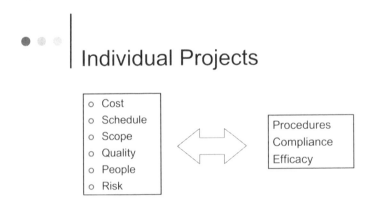

Figure 31

Managing multiple projects primarily focuses on the combined resource implications of several projects. As such, there is an effort to assure that the combined resource demand does not overrun, or under run, the organizational resource pool or affect the limits set upon that group of projects by the organization. Alternately, managing multiple projects could emphasize a close adherence of the combined cash flow of these projects with the organizational forecast for that group of projects. Portfolio imperatives could include the number of projects in the portfolio, percentage of funding for each group, or the sequencing of the deliverables of the projects in the portfolio pipeline (Figure 32). Although portfolio management includes managing projects in groups, sometimes managing multiple projects is used as a prelude to, or as a substitute for, program and portfolio management. It is an important point that these characterizations represent the enterprise viewpoint on the projects. The project team, on the other hand, should always focus on processes, knowledge areas, and activities, which bring about acceptable deliverables for their respective projects.

Issues that become necessary in managing multiple projects include resource sharing among projects, money sharing among projects, relationship of projects to each other in terms of milestones, deliverable swapping, and the strategic objectives to each project within that particular program/portfolio. Additionally, managing multiple projects that share the same resource pool, the same client, and the same stakeholders, highlights the need for sensitivity toward people issues such as communications, conflict management, leadership, and collaboration. To carry this concept one step further, the program/portfolio manager would do well by being attentive to people-related issues such as competency, work satisfaction, attrition, loyalty, harmony, and leadership.

Multiple Projects Considerations

- Combined Resource Demand
  - Overruns Organizational Pool
  - Under-runs Organizational Pool
  - Strains Portfolio Imperatives
- Combined Cash Flow Demand
  - Overruns Organizational Capability
  - Falls Short of Organizational Forecast

Figure 32

Chapter Summary. Although many organizations have some form of a prioritization model and some form of managing multiple projects within the organization, these models are usually narrative and debate based, and the management of the projects within the portfolio is judgment based and probably not formalized. A formalized and successful project portfolio management system must include sophisticated procedures for selecting and continuing the most relevant projects, and for methodically managing these projects to their respective point of logical conclusion.

By necessity, a formalized and comprehensive prioritization model would need to include quantitative components, even for those components that are usually considered to be difficult to quantify. The quantified indices should describe the attributes of the project deliverable and the value of that deliverable to the organization. The value of the project to the organization can be derived from two sets of indices: those describing the strategic utility of the deliverable, and those describing the financial viability of the deliverable. In organizations that strive to have one single portfolio for all of the organizational projects, another set of indices would be required by which the importance of different categories of projects will be signaled in the model.

Ultimately, the advantage of a formalized and all-inclusive model is that it makes explicit what is usually implicit in various meetings dealing with prioritization of projects. Consequently, upper management would not have to participate in prioritizing activities; rather, they would provide the rationale for the process, which will be handled by the portfolio management team. The net result is that upper management will be relieved of operational obligations in order to dedicate more time and energy to creating vision and strategic direction for the organization.

References

Allan, P. D. Improving the Consistency of Business Performance through Portfolio Management, presented at the Nineteenth Annual Meeting of the American Real Estate Society, Monterey, April 2-5, 2003, http://www.portfoliodecisions.com/res.htm

Archer, N. P. and G. Fereidoun. "An Integrated Framework for Project Portfolio Selection," International Journal of Project Management 17, 4, August 1999: 207-216.

Armstrong, C. "Project Portfolio Selection Methods," University of Wisconsin-Platteville, September 16, 2004.

Association for Project Management. Directing Change: A Guide to the Governance of Project Management, October 2005, http://www.apm.org.uk

Baker, J. R. and J. R. Freeland. "Recent Advances in R & D Benefit Measurement and Project Selection Methods," Management Science 21, 6 (1975): 1164-1175.

Berinato, S. "Do the Math," CIO magazine, IDG Publishers, October 1, 2001, http://www.cio.com/archive/100101/math.html

Bernoulli, D., 1738, as quoted in the "Exposition of a New Theory on the Measurement of Risk," Econometrica 22 (1954): 36.

Bohanec, M., et al. "Knowledge-Based Portfolio Analysis for Project Evaluation." Information & Management 28, 5, Amsterdam, May 1995: 293-302.

Boston Consulting Group, Inc. The Product Portfolio, 1970, www.bostonconsultinggroup.com

Brown, M. "Illuminating Patterns of Perception: An Overview of Q Methodology," Software Engineering Institute Technical Note. CMU/SEI-2004-TN-026, 2004.

Cable, J. H., et al. "Project Portfolio Earned Value Management Using Tree Maps," Project Management Institute Research Conference, London, July 2004, www.cs.umd.edu/hcil/treemap/PROJECT%20MANAGEMENT-ASPUBLISHED.pd

Case, J. The Open-Book Experience: Lessons from Over 100 Companies Who Successfully Transformed Themselves. Perseus Books, Reading, MA, 1998.

Center for Business Practices, Project Portfolio Management: A Benchmark of Current Business Practices, http://www.cbponline.com/research/ppm%20news.pd

Chin, G. "Agile Project Management: How to Succeed in the Face of Changing Project Requirements," AMACOM, New York, 2004.

CIO magazine. "The Powers that Should Be," September 15, 2002.

Cleland, D. I. and W. R. King, eds. Project Management Handbook. Van Nostrand Reinhold, New York, 1983.

Connor, D. R. Managing at the Speed of Change. Villard, New York, 1993.

Cooper, R. G. "Maximizing the Value of Our New Product Portfolio: Methods, Metrics & Scorecards," Presentation to the Stevens Alliance for Technology Management, 2001.

Cooper, R. G., S. J. Edgett and E. J. Kleinschmidt. "Best Practices for Managing R & D Portfolios," Research Technology Management 41, 4 (1998a): 20-33.

Cooper, R. G., S. J. Edgett and E. J. Kleinschmidt. "New Problems, New Solutions: Making Porfolio Management More Effective," Research Technology Management 43, 2 (2000): 18-33.

Cooper, R. G., S. J. Edgett and E. J. Kleinschmidt. "Portfolio Management in New Product Development: Lessons from the Leaders—I ," Research Technology Management 40, 5 (1997): 16-28.

Cooper, R. G., S. J. Edgett and E. J. Kleinschmidt. "Portfolio Management in New Product Development: Lessons from the Leaders—II," Research Technology Management 40, 6 (1997): 43-52.

Cooper, R. G., S. J. Edgett and E. J. Kleinschmidt. "Portfolio Management in New Product Development: Results of an Industry Practices Study," R & D Management 31, 4, October 2001, 361-381.

Cooper, R. G., S. J. Edgett and E. J. Kleinschmidt. Portfolio Management for New Products. Addison-Wesley, Reading, MA, 1998b.

Cooper, R. G., S. J. Edgett and E. J. Kleinschmidt. "Porfolio Management for New Products: Picking the Winners," Working Paper No. 11. Product Development Institute, Ontario, 2001.

Crawford, L., J. B. Hobbs and J. R. Turner. Project Categorization Systems Aligning Capability with Strategy for Better Results, Project Management Institute, Newtown Square, PA, 2005.

Cummings, J. "IT Portfolio Management," Network World 19, 13. Framingham, MA, April 1, 2002.

Datz, T. "Portfolio Management: How to Do It Right," CIO magazine, May 1, 2003, http://www.cio.com/archive/050103/portfolio.htm

De Reyck, B., et. al. "The Impact of Project Portfolio Management on Information Technology Projects," International Journal of Project Management 23, 7, October 2005, 23, 524-537.

Dickinson, M. W., A. C. Thornton and S. Graves. "Technology Portfolio Management: Optimizing Interdependent Projects Over Multiple Time Periods," IEEE Transactions on Engineering Management 48, 4, New York, November 2001, 18-27.

Dixon, M. ed. Association for Project Management. Body of Knowledge, 4th Edition. Association for Project Management, Buckinghamshire, UK, 2000.

Dinsmore, P. C. Winning in Business with Enterprise Project Management. The American Management Association Publications, New York, 1999.

Dobson, M. S. The Juggler's Guide to Managing Multiple Projects. Project Management Institute, Newtown Square, PA, 1999.

Duffy, T. "Keeping an Eye on IT," Network World, April 3, 2002, www.nwfusion.com/careers/2002/0304man.html

Essex, D. "In Search of ROI," PM Network, October 2005, 46-52.

Essex, D. "Software Tools Can Help You Put Your Agency's IT Investments in Order," Government Computer News, September 22, 2003.

Frame, J. D. Managing Projects in Organizations: How to Make the Best Use of Time, Techniques and People, 3rd Edition, Jossey Bass, San Francisco, 2003.

Gendron, G. "The Numbers on Open-Book Management," Inc. magazine, June 1998, http://www.inc.com/magazine/19980601/937.html

Ghasemzadeh, F. and N. P. Archer. "Project Portfolio Selection through Decision Support," Decision Support Systems 29, 1, Amsterdam, July 2000.

Goff, J. and E. Teach. "Analyze This: The Fundamentals of Portfolio Management are Being Applied to Corporate Technology Assets," CFO magazine, December 1, 2003.

Grant, T. A White Paper. "Evolution of the PMP: Agile Portfolio Management," July 2004, http://www.grantthornton.com/downloads/APM_whitepaper_100814.pdf

Groenveld, P. "Road-Mapping Integrates Business and Technology," Research Technology Management 40, 5, September 1997, 48-55.

Helin, A. F. and W. E. Souder. "Experimental Test of a Q-Sort Procedure for Prioritizing R & D Projects," IEEE Transactions on Engineering Management, November 1974.

Hill, G. M. The Complete Project Management Office Handbook. Auerbach Publications, Boca Raton, 2004.

Hoffman, T. "Balancing the IT Portfolio," Computerworld, February 10, 2003, www.computerworld.com/managementtopics.roi/story/0,10801,78267,78267,00.html

Howell, III, J. et al. "Implementing Portfolio Management: Integrating Process, People and Tools," Paper presented at the AAPG Annual Meeting, Houston, March 10-13, 2002, http://www.searchanddiscovery.com/documents/abstrcts/annual2002/data/200213annual/extended/46693.pdf

Hussey, D. Strategic Management from Theory to Implementation, 4th Edition. Butterworth-Heinemann, Oxford, UK, 1998.

Kendall, G. I. and S. C. Rollins. Advanced Project Management and the PMO, Multiplying ROI at Warp Speed. J. Ross Publishing, Boca Raton, 2003.

Kerzner, H. Project Management: A Systems Approach to Planning, Scheduling and Controlling, 8th Edition. John Wiley and Sons, Inc., Hoboken, 2003.

Kerzner, H. Strategic Planning for Project Management Using a Project Management Maturity Model. John Wiley and Sons, Inc., New York, 2001.

Knutson, J. Succeeding in Project-Driven Organizations: People, Processes and Politics. John Wiley and Sons, Inc., New York, 2001.

Kodukula P. Project Portfolio Management: A Practitioner's Guide to Excellence. J. Ross Publishing, Boca Raton, 2005.

Kotter, J. P. "Leading Change—Why Transformation Efforts Fail," Harvard Business Review 73, 2 (1995): 59-67.

Liberatore, M. J. and G. J. Titus. "The Practice of Management Science in R & D Project Management," Management Science 29, 8 (1983): 962-974.

Lynn, D. "Enterprise Portfolio Analysis Tools," January 6, 2003, http://www.metagroup.com.us/displayArticle.do?oid=41473

Markowitz, H. "Foundations of Portfolio Theory," The Journal of Finance 46, 2, June 1991, 469-477.

Markowitz, H. "Portfolio Selection," The Journal of Finance 7, 1, March 1952, 77-91.

Markowitz, H. "The Early History of Portfolio Theory: 1600-1960," Financial Analysts Journal 55, 4, July/August 1999, 5-16.

Markowitz, H. Portfolio Selection: Efficient Diversification of Investments, Cowles Foundation Monograph #16 (Wiley 1959), reprinted in a 2nd Edition, with Markowitz's hindsight comments on several chapters and with an additional bibliography supplied by Mark Rubinstein (Blackwell 1991).

Martino, J. P. "Project Selection," in Project Management Toolbox Tools and Techniques for the Practicing Project Manager. Milosevic, D. Z. and John Wiley and Sons, Inc., Hoboken (2003): 19-66.

Maynard, S. D. Independent Study: "Integrated Approach to Product and Process Re-engineering," University of Wisconsin-Platteville, 2005.

McDonough, III, E. F. and F. C. Spital, "Managing Project Portfolios," Research Technology Management 46, 3, May/June 2003, 40-46,

McFarland, F. W. "IT Governance and Portfolio Management Overview," CSC World, http://www.csc.com/cscworld

Meredith, J. R. and S. J. Mantel, Jr. Project Management: A Managerial Approach, 6th Edition. John Wiley and Sons, Inc., Hoboken, 2006.

META Group. "The Business of IT Portfolio Management: Balancing Risk, Innovation and ROI," January 2002, http://www.metagroup.com/metaview/mv0520.html

Mikkola, J. H. "Portfolio Management of R & D Projects: Implications for Innovation Management," Technovation 21, 7, Amsterdam, July 2001.

Milosevic, D. Z. Project Management Toolbox Tools and Techniques for the Practicing Project Manager. John Wiley and Sons, Inc., Hoboken, 2003.

Morris, P. and A. Jamieson. Translating Corporate Strategy into Project Strategy Realizing Corporate Strategy through Project Management. Project Management Institute, Newtown Square, PA, 2004.

Organization for Economic Co-operation and Development: "OECD Principles of Corporate Governance," 2004, http://www.oecd.org

Pennypacker, J. and P. Sepate. "Real Alignment: Portfolio Management Capabilities Allow Organizations to Better Control and Manage Assets, Increasing Responsiveness, Revenues and Adaptability," Projects@Work, December 10, 2003.

Peterson, M. and T. Myers. Collaborative Enterprise Portfolio Management: Increasing Value Returns through Performing Innovation. J. Ross Publishing, Boca Raton, 2005.

Pinto, J. K., D. Cleland and D. Slevin. The Frontiers of Project Management Research. Project Management Institute, Newtown Square, PA, 2003.

Platje, A., H. Seidel and S. Wadman. "Project and Portfolio Planning Cycle," International Journal of Project Management 12, 2, May 1994, 100-106.

Project Management Institute. A Guide to the Project Management Body of Knowledge, 3rd Edition. Project Management Institute, Newtown Square, PA, 2004.

Project Management Institute. A Guide to the Project Management Body of Knowledge. Project Management Institute, Newtown Square, PA, 2000.

Project Management Institute. Organizational Project Management Maturity Model Knowledge Foundation. Project Management Institute, Newtown Square, PA, 2003.

Project Management Institute. The Standard for Portfolio Management. Project Management Institute, Newtown Square, PA, 2006a.

Project Management Institute. The Standard for Program Management. Project Management Institute, Newtown Square, PA, 2006b.

Pugh, G. "Steps to Successful Change Management," Business Processes: The Magazine for Members of the National Computing Center, www.pmi-chicagoland.org/news_events/Presentations/PMIChicago_PPM%20&%20Cultural%20Change_dec2003.ppt

Rad, P. F. and G. Levin. Achieving Project Management Success Using Virtual Teams. J. Ross Publishing, Boca Raton, 2003.

Rad, P. F. and G. Levin. The Advanced Project Management Office. St. Lucie Press, Boca Raton, 2002.

Rad, P. F. and G. Levin. Metrics for Project Managers' Formalized Approaches. Management Concepts, Vienna, VA, 2006.

Raz, T. "An Iterative Screening Methodology for Selecting Project Alternatives," Project Management Journal, Decemeber 1997, 34-39.

Satay, T. L. The Analytic Hierarchy Process. McGraw-Hill Company, New York, 1980.

Scheinberg, M. V. "Planning of Portfolio Projects," Project Management Journal 23, 2, June 1992, 31-37.

Scheinberg, M. V. and A. Stretton. "Multiproject Planning: Tuning Portfolio Indices," International Journal of Project Management 12, 2, May 1994, 107-114.

Schmidt, R. L. and J. Freeland. "Recent Progress in Modeling R & D Project-Selection Processes," IEEE Transactions on Engineering Management 39, 2, (1992): 189-201.

Sharpe, W. F. "Capital Asset Prices: A Theory of Market Equilibrium under Conditions of Risk," The Journal of Finance 19, 3, (1964): 425-442.

Souder, W. E. "Utility and Perceived Acceptability of R & D Project-Selection Models," Management Science 19, 12, August 1973, 1384-1394.

Stack, J. The Great Game of Business. Currency Doubleday, New York, 1992.

Stephenson, W. The Study of Behavior: Q-technique and Its Methodology, University of Chicago Press, (Chicago): 1953.

Tobin, J. "Liquidity Preference as Behavior Toward Risk," The Review of Economic Studies 67, February 1958, http://cowles.econ.yale.edu/P/cp/p101a/p0118.pdf

Van Donk, D. and J. Riezebos. "Exploring the Knowledge Inventory in Project-Based Organisations: A Case Study," International Journal of Project Management 23, January 2005, 75-83.

Varghese, C. "Resolving the Process Paradox: A Strategy for Launching Meaningful Process Improvement," Cost Engineering 46, 11, November 2004, 13-21.

U.S. Government Accountability Office. "Selection Processes," http://www.gao.gov/new.items/d0449.pdf

Walsh, S. "Portfolio Management for the Commercialization of Advanced Technologies," Engineering Management Journal 13, 1, March 2001, 33

Wheelwright, S. C. and K. B. Clark. "Creating Project Plans to Focus Product Development," Harvard Business Review 70, 2, (1992): 67-83.

Wysocki, R. K. and R. McGarry. Effective Project Management, 3rd Edition. John Wiley and Sons, Inc. (Indianapolis) 2003.

Index